How to Heal Your Nightmares

Meg Renfri Bartlett

Book Editor: James Oliver
Cover Design: Evgeniia Gurcheva

Published by Meg Bartlett in Minneapolis, Minnesota, USA
Contact: meg@megbartlett.com
Website: https://megbartlett.com/

Paperback ISBN: 979-8-9920116-0-9

Library of Congress Control Number: 2025901858

First Edition, February 2025

Printed by IngramSpark

For the little girl who saw demons,
I know now that I have always loved you.

Disclaimer: Some of the names of individuals within this book have been changed to protect their privacy. Additionally, while I believe everything in this book to be true to the best of my memory, I acknowledge that it's possible for two people to go through the exact same experience but recall it differently. Memories are formed as they pass through an individual's unique filter which is shaped by the totality of their life's experiences, emotions, thoughts, and soul signature of which every person on the planet has their own unique combination. This book details a single perception of the world: my own.

Content Warning: Within these pages you'll find some humorous moments, but this is, ultimately, a book about nightmares—both the ones I've experienced in dreamtime and the ones I've lived through. That said, this book includes memories and thoughts of suicidal ideation, physical abuse, sexual abuse, and other difficult moments.

If you are a survivor of your own difficult moments or are currently experiencing one, help is available.

Call or text "988" for the U.S. Suicide & Crisis Lifeline

If you are a veteran, call or text "988" then press "1" for assistance or visit https://www.veteranscrisisline.net/

Contents

Introduction

A bolt of lightning pierced the rain-whipped waves, illuminating the depths beneath the ship's belly to expose the shadow of a colossal monstrosity. Its massive, snake-like body undulated in a rhythmic, circular pattern beneath the churning surface of the sea. While the creature could easily devour the entire craft, destruction was not its intent—it relished the stench of my fear. An ancient terror emanated from the beast, echoing louder and louder across the frozen expanse of my mind as the tendrils of a black, etheric ooze curled around my chest and through the passageways of my lungs. The familiar sensation of overwhelming panic poured into my limbs, drowning me in its suffocating ichor.

CRACK!

The air sizzled and danced with electricity as a clap of thunder rolled across the waves, snapping me into the present moment. Racing across the deck, I launched myself up the stairs that led to the bridge looking for help but the helm was empty. Acknowledgment brutally collided with dread as I realized I was the only person aboard this vessel. A mouthful of bile rose up, stinging my tongue with the acrid blackness of despair. I swallowed, forcing it back down into the frothing witch's brew in my stomach, and tried to harden my resolve.

A quick assessment from the bridge provided little comfort. Steering the ship was practically inconceivable in this tempest, the lack of starlight rendered navigation nearly impossible, and the mast had started to splinter under the weight of unmanaged sails. Any last remnants of hope I'd had washed away with the pounding sheets of rain. I was alone at sea with the king of earthly demons. My light went out.

The coolness of a shadow loomed across the quarterdeck and as I turned to greet it my eyes took in the rising wall of water that stood twenty years high. The rogue wave from countless nightmares was back and though it had never completely enveloped me before, I knew now that it was unavoidable. Tonight, it stood as a harbinger of doom and there, within the wall of black water, shone the calculated, beady eyes of the monster in the depths—a biblical behemoth.

Leviathan.

It extended its head out from the wave, slowly reaching toward me as rivulets of water cascaded down its black scales. The beast's yellow eyes, vaguely familiar, commanded my limbs to slacken and still. Caught in its spell, I almost recognized the hidden memory that shimmered within those orbs, a deep fear that I had buried long ago. Though I didn't fully comprehend its significance, a profound sense of knowing clicked into place and I knew, *I knew*, this monster had been waiting to meet me.

Then, in a moment of brief lucidity, I realized that my recurring Creature-in-the-Depths Nightmare had been holding a key all along. The answers were just there, dancing within the knowledge of those glowing yellow pupils but before full recognition could set in, the leviathan opened its maw and mercifully devoured me whole, plunging us both into the watery abyss below.

I had met my maker.

(*Exploration and Interpretation, Creature-in-the-Depths Nightmare*)

This is a book about nightmares—both the ones I've dreamt and the ones I've lived through—and how I used their wisdom to heal my life.

Nightmares are a subset of dreams categorized by the feeling of fear and, like dreams, nightmares are an expression of our internal conversation. They can be experienced through any combination of physical, psychological, and spiritual senses such as visual imagery, sound, touch, taste, smell, emotion, intuition, and even simply the sense of knowing. While nightmares are most common in childhood many people can develop recurring or frequent nightmares in adulthood as well. If left unacknowledged, recurring nightmares can become debilitating and are often observed in conjunction with a combination of other symptoms such as sleep difficulties or insomnia, problems with memory and concentration, psychological stress or illness, trouble regulating mood and emotions, a declining quality of personal connections and relationships, and even suppressed immune system function or physical illness. The key to healing our nightmares (the ones we dream and the ones we live through) begins with understanding that nightmares are a symptom, and all symptoms have a root cause that can be healed.

Symptoms are messengers of the mind-body-energy system that creates our human experience and their message is always the same: find, acknowledge, and work with the root. When we listen to our symptoms, acknowledge our roots, and work to begin healing them, our symptoms (the messengers) are no longer needed. Our dreamtime nightmares are an observation of our internal fear-based conversation. Therefore, our nightmares hold the unique information we each individually need in order for us to identify, acknowledge, and work with our roots to heal the nightmares we've lived through.

For twenty years of my life, I experienced consistent and recurring nightmares with frequent episodes of sleep paralysis—a temporary state of consciousness one enters just before waking often characterized by the sensation of complete or partial paralysis and feeling deeply afraid. Over time, I developed a fear of sleep entirely and attempted to avoid my nightmares by suppressing them with alcohol and marijuana. I found that while substances did lessen the immediate impact of my nightmares, they only prolonged the inevitable and buried the fear that needed to be felt.

Substances also made it more difficult for me to fall asleep and stay asleep, submerging my mind-body-energy system into a state of perpetual fatigue that began to expose a myriad of other symptoms I had purposefully avoided acknowledging throughout my life. My symptoms (again, the messages I was sending myself) included mental illness, high blood pressure, a decline in the quality of my relationships, difficulty concentrating at work, painful migraines that would send me home early, and unstoppable emotional outbursts that often descended into intense panic attacks. At first, I adopted the typical societal narrative that I should just push through the symptoms, take a pain pill to get me through the day and hope the symptoms would go away on their own. But when I moved to Seattle in November of 2016, I began to acknowledge just how overwhelming my symptoms were becoming and the deep impact they were having on my life. I knew that something needed to change.

I had just completed a five-year enlistment in the Marine Corps (an extra year was devoted to the special schooling for my job or MOS—Military Occupational Specialty) and I assumed that these symptoms, along with my nightmares, were just a result of my deployment to Afghanistan the year prior. As I settled into my new life in Seattle, I put any ingrained, pride-based narratives aside for a moment and began working regularly with a psychological therapist to address my symptoms in what I thought would be a quick and efficient manner. I was a Marine, goddammit, and I figured I'd just find out whatever was causing it and beat the source back into submission!

Boy was I wrong.

As I waded into the murky waters of my life's history I discovered that my symptoms and nightmares had existed well before I entered the service and that, while I did have service-connected PTSD, something else was lingering in the depths. The deeper I dove, the clearer it became that the thundering echoes of mortar fire were just the tip of the iceberg and lying at the bottom of my hollowed-out heart were two horrific memories I had buried as well as the foundational beliefs that I was a guilty soul and completely undeserving of life. It wasn't the nightmares themselves that were causing my suffering, it was the devastating, raw, unprocessed, and unacknowledged moments that I had buried deep within my subconscious in order to survive the horrors of my childhood. It was my roots.

Our roots are the foundational moments that shape us. They're often the first memories that surface when someone asks about our life story and are usually tied to the people that have impacted us the most. Our roots are often emotionally charged and highlight the major, transitional events of our lives. Most of our roots are processed without much conscious thought like graduating high school and setting out on our own as a young adult or marrying a partner and beginning to build a life together. But some roots carry a heavy weight with them and can become stuck, mired in the grips of an emotional depth we don't currently have the capacity to comprehend. The roots that get stuck are almost always fear-based and are centered in the most difficult or traumatic moments of our lives.

Some fear-based roots *can* be processed quickly, like watching a scary movie and only needing to sleep with the lights on for a week before resuming a natural sleep pattern (as I did after seeing the creepy vampires in *Salem's Lot* as a teenager), but other fear-based roots halt their processing entirely, freezing the root moment in time along with the emotions, thoughts, and even physical sensations present in the experience. We do this not because we are failing ourselves in some way, but because we simply don't have the tools, feeling of safety, verbiage, or understanding needed at the time of the initial impact to fully comprehend and process the experiences. It's as if we're saving the work for later when we find the resources and words to make sense of it. Sometimes we save our most difficult roots for a long while until their memories begin to dig a well of tension in the center of the root event and, eventually, we develop symptoms to draw our attention to them—we send ourselves messages. Like an ingrown hair that festers under the surface of the skin, unprocessed roots can begin to show their pain whether we want them to or not, asking for us, through the language of symptoms, to pay attention and do the inner work necessary to resolve them.

As I dove into my roots in Seattle with the assistance of psychological guidance I began to notice that the emotions I felt in my nightmares were identical to the emotions I felt when exploring my frozen roots in therapy. A deep sense of knowing began to bubble up from within me, a knowing that this uncanny resemblance was more than mere coincidence. I followed my gut and began recording and observing my nightmares in an attempt to discover the link between them and my waking life. Over time, I accumulated a significant amount of personal data and discovered that the connection between our nightmares and our unprocessed roots contains the unique wisdom necessary for us to heal.

That single decision—to intentionally acknowledge my nightmares—changed me forever.

Nightmares aren't a punishment from the universe (though they can certainly feel like it sometimes), nightmares depict our frozen roots and contain the right combination of personal knowledge and observation that we each need in order to pick up the integration process where we left it off and move through the experience once and for all.

Nightmares show us where dissonance exists within ourselves so that we can be empowered to do something about it. They highlight the moments of our lives that have created an overarching narrative of fear that, over time, stymies our capacity for love and joy. They're the internal messengers, the symptoms, that work on behalf of our greater selves, laying out a healing pathway, showing us what needs to be seen, and encouraging us to be the change we wish to see in our own lives.

Our nightmares exist to help us heal.

The word "healing" can mean many different things to many different people. To me, healing is the process of returning to wholeness. When we first enter this world, we are perfect beings, completely existing in the totality of our true essence as babies, but as we move into the force of linear time, our true nature becomes convoluted. As we grow and age, we try on different societal, fa-milial, and religious narratives for size. Some of them are beneficial structures but many are limiting, and we find ourselves covered in various dialogues and expressions of fear. We're not doing any-thing wrong here, it's just a fact of the human experience, but I believe that each soul's responsibility on this planet is to become consciously aware of the limiting, fear-based narratives we've taken on, do the work necessary to actively work through them, and uncover our innate source of self one layer at a time, returning to wholeness.

Healing begins with the conscious acknowledgment that some-thing needs to change and is followed by action to support and facilitate that change. While it would be nice to have a step-by-step healing formula written within this book, healing is not a one-size-fits-all process, nor is it a linear one. Like the stages of grief, healing is a unique combination of physical, psychological, emotional, and spiritual changes that lead us forward in the way we each need. Its intent is not to return to the way things were before—we can never un-know what we now know, un-feel what we have felt, or un-see what we have seen—but rather, healing is the choice to peel back the limiting layers and find a new, loving way to live with the unique circumstances this life has given us.

Some people heal quickly and efficiently, acknowledging and processing their major roots like any other experience as they go. Some people take months, years, or even several decades to process their roots and heal, repressing and avoiding the truth until their nightmares or symptoms run rampant, demanding to be seen and dealt with. And yet, many people lock themselves within a perpetual pattern of avoidance, growing old and passing on without ever listening to the wisdom of their internal selves, experiencing a lifetime plagued by unending nightmares, difficulties and other issues that never resolve simply because they're unwilling to change.

I was one of the people that ignored my truth for a significant amount of time before working with my roots, suffering through the language of symptoms and nightmares for two decades before finally acknowledging that something needed to change. By the time I acted on this realization and sought out psychological help in 2017, I was close to the bottom of the major depression well. I had avoided my symptoms for so long that my mind had started to avoid itself, leaving me barely able to recall much of my existence before joining the military. Whole years of my memory were gone, replaced by a feeling of nothingness and the desire to believe that my formative years were largely uneventful. I had cut myself off from my foundational roots so viscerally after experiencing pain in such profound ways that I preferred to see nothing at all.

As I began the grueling process of reintegrating myself, I began to remember who I truly was, not the mask I wore, and what I had experienced, working with my memories one at a time in the order that they surfaced—my unique healing pathway. The first major root I consciously held was a memory that I had deeply wounded my younger brother. We had been children at the time (I was six and he was four) but I had taken on the weight of responsibility reserved for eldest siblings and the knowledge of what I had done left profound imprints of self-loathing and guilt upon my conscience that grew with me into adulthood.

Once I acknowledged and began working through that first frozen memory, the burden of guilt that I had carried since childhood started to ease up. My emotional capacity expanded, and I learned that it was safe to feel my way through everything I had locked away because now I had the tools, assistance, and know-how to process it. But as the load of that first frozen root lightened, I realized it wasn't the only one I carried. My other roots began to thaw, loosening up the years of physical and psychological abuse that defined my upbringing until I unearthed the deepest root of all. It had been waiting in the depths for me to develop the capacity to hold it and now that I was finally walking down the healing pathway, the memories of sexual abuse I had endured as a young girl clicked into place.

Suddenly, my recurring Creature-in-the-Depths Nightmare made sense. The leviathan, my monster of a truth, the thing I knew that I didn't want to know, had been circling below the emotional storm that permeated much of my life, waiting for a moment of recognition as it emerged from the waves. Not only did the imagery itself make sense, but the emotions most prevalent in that nightmare were identical to those I felt when thinking about my roots: terrified, alone, and frozen in fear. Someone that I trusted, someone that I loved, someone that was supposed to love and protect me as a child had done a terrible thing and I had remained locked inside a state of suffering ever since. My nightmares had been trying to guide me to dig up my own truth the whole time. The acknowledgment of my unprocessed roots initiated my healing experience and in the years that followed I unearthed the lost puzzle pieces to complete the picture. All the while my nightmares shifted and changed with me as I understood more and more of my own truth, guiding me with their unending wisdom.

Through this process, I have made peace with my nightmares and befriended the monsters, now only experiencing them occasionally and without recurrence. I no longer suffer from Major Depressive Disorder (MDD), the symptoms of my Complex Post-Traumatic Stress Disorder (C-PTSD) are almost nonexistent, I rarely experience the panic attacks that used to rule my life, and I no longer wake gasping for breath from terrifying episodes of sleep paralysis. The best part though is that I have conquered my fear of sleep and have found the joy of dreams again! Today, I help people all over the world interpret and understand their own dreams and nightmares, guide them to their roots and assist them in identifying their unique healing pathway. My cup is overflowing and all of this I attribute to the wisdom of my own nightmares, the therapists, friends, and found family that listened to them, my incessant drive to understand and heal myself, and the desire to live my life as a whole, loving, and authentic being.

This book explores the depths of my story and details exactly how I have healed my nightmares. While most of this is a memoir, I've included a couple of sections in the back to add some extra depth and assist you along the way. The *Exploration and Interpretation* section breaks down the nightmares you'll find throughout these pages with my style of interpretation and notable takeaways, *A Brief Compendium of Common Nightmares* contains common interpretations partnered with questions to guide you towards each nightmare's wisdom, and lastly, we have the *Books That Changed My Life* which may be beneficial to you as well. Take a moment to reference any of these sections at any time—you may find them helpful as you come across reflections of your own nightmares.

I'll be honest with you, working with nightmares can be brutal at times but it's always worth it. All nightmares are rooted somewhere in waking life, therefore, all nightmares can be resolved and healed in waking life. As you dive in, it's important to note that while your nightmares can show you what to heal, it's up to you to seek out and enact your own resolution. There are many sources of information and services for healing out there (physical, psychological, emotional, and spiritual) but these pieces of information and services are only truly effective when *you* follow through with them. A doctor can perform surgery on your leg after an accident but only your dedication to physical therapy can help you walk freely again. A therapist can help you psychologically and emotionally find internal peace but only if you share with them your truth and fully participate in the work and practice your toolbox. And a reiki practitioner can balance your chakras or clear your energy but if someone cuts you off in traffic on the way home and you roll down your window to make sure the offender can actually *see* your middle finger as you stick it out the window to yell at them to fuck off then you might find your solar plexus and sacral chakras in chaos again—whoops!

The point is that it's entirely up to you to heal. It's your choice to unearth and enact your own healing wisdom within this life and, at the end of the day, it's your responsibility to show up for yourself. My nightmares were the part of me that wanted to heal and even though it took me a long time to listen, they were so, so very glad when I did.

This is a book about nightmares and how to use their wisdom to heal your life.

You are your own greatest catalyst for change.

You are the healer you need the most and your nightmares have been waiting to show you what they (what you) already know.

It is safe to see. It is safe to know. You have gotten this far, and you are capable of going even further. Take your nightmares by the hand, look them in the eye, and move forward one step at a time. Your nightmares are here to help.

1

The Formation of a Secret Keeper

I used to be terrified of sleeping in the dark so my parents would let me leave the bathroom light on across the hall each night as I drifted off. I'd beg them to leave it on *all night*, but every time I woke in the wee hours of the morning I'd find myself surrounded by darkness and the ghouls who roamed the hallways would be waiting for me, thriving on the stench of my fear and the echoes of my nightmares. The sounds of wet, squishing footsteps on the carpet and the scrape of long, sharp nails across the walls belonging to creatures from distant realms filled me with dread. I never wanted to look at them, the monsters, but the energy of their presence always commanded my gaze and I'd find myself with the covers pulled up to my nose staring at them in horror whether I wanted to or not.

What I remember most are their eyes. Most had glowing yellow eyes but some were red, and occasionally an oozing, gray creature with sunken black pits in its skull would visit and watch me sleep from the doorway. That's all the creatures did, watch me, but it was terrifying nonetheless. Over time, they became familiar and I could easily identify the regulars from those who had just dropped in to see what all the fuss was about. I tried to do what my parents asked—to grow up and get over them—but the monsters were always there waiting, night after night, nightmare after nightmare. They remained.

Eventually, I learned to stop talking about the demons who cajoled in the hall and took matters into my own hands, trying to make them leave the only way a little Catholic girl knew how: with the power of angels. With my allowance and chore money, I started collecting little ceramic cherubs called Dreamsicles (the irony is not lost on me today) and I'd arrange them on the singular bookshelf of my twin bed's headboard, pretending that they were guardians divinely sent by God to protect me. I enjoyed adding to my collection and before long I began asking my mom if I could tag along to the Kennedy Mall in our hometown of Dubuque, Iowa so I could dip into the Hallmark store and see which new angels were waiting for me. I had a wonderful menagerie of baby angels in every form imaginable!

I had angels that held stars, angels playing the piano, angels singing songs, angels of both genders (determined by a stereotypical pink or blue ribbon in their hair), fat angels and skinny angels, flying angels and sitting angels, an angel in a snow globe, an angel music box... you get the picture. The angels actually *did* help, if nothing but to make me feel like I wasn't quite so alone but the monsters were still there each night roaming the hall, lingering in my doorway during the deepest hours, whispering to me in strange, ancient tongues, and penetrating their fear-inducing energy through my purchased defenses. The pillow over my head could never quite shut them out.

One night I felt a different presence arriving in the dreamspace. Shaking myself from the depths of sleep into an in-between state of semi-consciousness (perhaps today I'd say it was a moment of lucidity) I spied a small black cat in the doorway. She stood looking at me with bright green eyes, scanning my bedroom and taking in her surroundings. I felt no fear from her and intuitively knew that her observations were beneficial, unlike the spying or leering gestures of the ghouls. Satisfied, she sauntered silently into the middle of my room and gingerly sat back on her hind legs, cocking her head to the side to then assess *me*. My curiosity peaked. I slowly sat up in bed and after a few more moments of assessing each other, she began speaking directly to my soul beyond the concept of verbal language. The cat told me that she came from a place called *the astral plane*. My angels had called her here to help explain some things to me because I was having a hard time hearing them.

She continued and clarified that I didn't need to be afraid of the demons and ghouls because they were observers only. It was impossible for them to physically harm or interact with me in any way because if they did they'd be breaking the rules of the universe. She said the monsters were just curious and, though they were hungry and salivating at the thought of eating the pile of secrets I held inside my heart, they valued their freedom more than the meal I might make. This whole home was full of secrets and the energetic call of our cache beckoned many creatures here who were curious and interested in them.

The cat paused to look behind me at my angels for a moment before translating that they were encouraging me to let go of some of the secrets I held because the release would lessen the weight of my fear and deter the monsters from my room, allowing me to sleep and experience the joy of dreams again.

(*Exploration and Interpretation, The Cat and the Ghouls*)

I understood exactly what she was saying about the secrets in our home, but even though it made sense, I just couldn't do it. As a child, many of the adults in my life praised me for acting "so grown up" and took to confiding in me, trusting me with their secrets, the knowledge of their inner workings, and conversations that my friends and siblings weren't privy to. I was given responsibilities that far exceeded my age and though I gladly took them on, it wasn't because I could actually handle them, it was one of the only ways I ever received praise and felt valued—it was how I experienced love. The pride and sense of belonging that I felt in being seen as my mother's "mini-me" far exceeded my fear of the ghouls and demons in my nightmares. As the first-born child to my parents and the first grandchild of my extended family, the pressure to perform and appear as adult-like as possible started early and when I successfully (by their standards) operated within the defined box of our complicated family system, I received the sense of worth I craved. By the time I was six years old, I understood the role that had been assigned to me and that our familial definition of success was determined by one's comprehensibility and control of information.

Information was a precious resource in my early environment, almost like a type of currency, and the keeping of secrets was what kept the cogs of our family system turning with its ability to both support and destroy the individuals it regarded.

All information existed to keep the family's image in good standing. Any information that would negatively affect the image of the system was dismissed and buried. Information could be used as both a defensive mechanism and as a weapon, depending on who wielded it. No one trusted each other, not even my parents in their relationship, and it was a known fact that trusting someone could eventually lead to pain if they proved themselves disloyal and it was imperative to avoid pain at all costs. We were a very pain-averse bunch which is ironic because, looking back, everyone existed in their own storm of unending suffering which was either caused by the intentional miscommunication of information or by burying important information that would have created room for peace and healing. My family system was a closed-loop designed to keep us locked within what we knew because change was terrifying.

I remember some parts of my childhood fondly and I know that I laughed a lot but the ever-present control of information made it, ultimately, a painful one. To my knowledge, my parents originally only wanted one girl and one boy which they received in that order (myself and my first sibling, my brother, who has asked to remain anonymous in this book) before the surprise pregnancy and birth of a second sibling, Sasha. Down the road we also adopted my third sibling when I was in high school, a distant cousin. All four of us loved each other but we also existed within our closed-loop system of pain and, therefore, enacted pain upon each other often.

Our parents had a lot of unresolved wounds and they'd take them out on each other, as well as myself and my siblings, through various forms of abuse. My dad usually expressed his pain through short but violent bursts of physical aggression that left red welts upon our bodies while my mom expressed hers through psychological control and emotional manipulation which contributed to the formation of a hyper-responsible, guilt-focused narrative within me. My siblings and I quickly learned how to take the pain we'd been given (physical, psychological, and emotional) and redistribute it to each other in the ways we observed from our parents and experienced ourselves which just kept the cycle going. It was a forbidden thing to mention our individual pain and, if we did, we belittled each other's perceptions of the events, gaslighting each other into believing that it really wasn't as bad as we'd made it seem—we were always just exaggerating—because if we talked about our pain then we'd have to look at it and none of us really knew what to do after that. So we kept fighting and hurting and belittling and screaming at each other and as the years wore on the secrets eventually ate us all alive.

My coping mechanism at the time was to quickly stake a position as my parents' confidant. If I knew what they were thinking and feeling before it spiraled out of control I felt like I could predict their emotional weather and prevent the storm. As a result, I developed a sense of hyper-responsibility at a very young age for what I said and how I said it, understanding that my words could carry significant weight. My dad always used to say that, "sticks and stones will break your bones but words can never hurt you," but I knew that was a lie because I could say shit that would make him explode with rage and clearly hurt a part of him he avoided. I learned what words could trigger specific emotions and memories and that the information they conveyed could be powerful.

The encouraged and necessary keeping of secrets and other sensitive information in our family system not only showed me that I needed to avoid pain at all costs but laid a foundational desire for me to understand how to use those secrets to my advantage in order to survive and avoid conflict. I started listening intently to

the conversations of the adults around me when I was in kindergarten and whenever a hint of a secret came up I'd focus my gaze
on the individual it concerned, taking note of how they reacted
to the exposure of their secret and mentally jotting down their
signs of agitation, anxiety, and/or anger. By the time I was in grade
school, I had learned how to read my parents' body language and
emotional state well and was able to manipulate their behavior in
return (to some extent) for what I thought was everyone's benefit.
I soothed them whenever possible, helped them retain their own
secrets when the need arose, and hid from them when I was unable
to salvage the situation or when they fought with each other. I kept
many of mom's extra purchases a secret from dad who would be
furious that she'd put it on her credit card. I kept dad's secrets when
he exploded with rage and took it out on us physically because
mom would be horrified to learn that when she left for a week
on a mission trip to Haiti that I had to beg dad not to kill Sasha
as he beat the literal shit out of them in the entryway like an old,
dusty doormat while wearing nothing but their favorite yellow
rain boots—Sasha was two years old. I even kept my Oma's secrets
when she would come over to babysit and give us bags of gummy
bears and other extra sweets because if we didn't keep it a secret
from our parents *she'd never be allowed to see us again* and we
didn't want that, did we? But most of all I learned to keep my own
secrets because no one could know half of everything or our family
would fall apart and it would all be my fault. Everyone had a secret,
everyone was hiding, and no one wanted to acknowledge that they
were in pain because then they'd be forced to consciously feel it.

The easiest secret for me to keep was the knowledge that I
had sexually abused my brother when I was six and he was four.

Sometimes we were hiding in his closet or behind my bed and in every scenario my pants would be missing while his were usually on—I never wanted him to take his off because that's not how you did it, that's not how I learned. The first time we were caught, mom told us that under no circumstances were we allowed to talk about this with anybody. We had to keep it a secret and I was never to do it again. I don't remember the exact words she used but I do remember the look of sheer, adult-sized horror scrawling itself across her face and knowing that I was the one who placed it there. The emotional weight of those unremembered words left me feeling profoundly dirty, wrong, and disgusting. I felt like a nasty bug that needed to be squashed under a boot. I was six years old and it was my first lesson in how to embody self-hatred. I didn't understand why it was wrong because someone else was showing it to me, but I thought something like, *if my* mom *thinks I'm this bad and disgusting, then I truly must be and I don't want anyone else to hate me.* The secret of the closet incidents easily ended up in my memory's graveyard as just another memory to avoid. Today, I don't remember if I ever told my mom in those moments *why* I was molesting him but there was a feeling that she was deeply terrified of what she knew it meant: that someone we loved, an adult we knew, was doing something unspeakable to me. But in our family we kept secrets for a reason and that reason, at all costs, was to avoid pain.

To my recollection I only ever received two detentions in school despite being frequently grounded at home. The first occurred in the second week of kindergarten when I grabbed my friend

Matthew by the face and kissed him full on the mouth in the middle of the hallway on the way back from gym class. Our principal, an old nun, was standing right behind me when I did it. After school I found myself sitting in her office waiting for my mom to pick me up and trying to explain through my tears how confused I was because my parents always kissed each other hello and goodbye and they were friends too. Wasn't that how friends said hello? When my mom arrived she laughed it off and told the principal we weren't staying for detention because I was a kindergartener and that was ridiculous. We drove off to get some ice cream—a small chocolate chip cookie dough blizzard from Dairy Queen for me and a medium cherry-dipped vanilla cone for her—which always fixed everything.

The second detention I received was sometime in the second grade. We'd just returned from recess and I was sitting next to my best friend Gwen trying my hardest to focus on basic fractions when my gut gurgled. Suddenly, and without warning, the loudest, longest fart you can imagine erupted out of my asshole! Silence fell upon the classroom as Mrs. Johnson slowly turned around to look at me with shock and before I could stop myself I started laughing those deep, full-bellied laughs that are most contagious. The entire class descended into hysterical laughter, kids fell off their seats, and pandemonium ensued. Mrs. Johnson was a wonderful teacher but I had rattled my classmates nearly as much as my fart had rattled the old single-pane awning windows and as the minutes passed by, still full of chaos, her mirth transformed into frustration at our collective lack of composure. Eventually, the class calmed down but Gwen and I struggled to keep ourselves in check throughout the rest of the day, breaking into frequent fits of giggles that brought the rest of the class with us again and again. We both received detention for creating an unparalleled classroom disturbance, and later had to scrawl out something like, "I will not laugh out of turn," in our notebooks until our hands cramped. (My suggestion to write, "I will not fart in class" was deemed too inappropriate for Catholic school.)

While I truly laugh about these memories today, they really laid some negative groundwork at the time and I walked away from my detentions with the belief that good things, like love and laughter, can be a cause for punishment if not suppressed. This belief was doubled down in other experiences both at home and at school where I was frequently told that I was too much, too wild, too loud, and that I needed to learn how to keep myself in check. But the narrative differed and some behaviors that were acceptable at home with my family were not acceptable at school, and vice versa. Navigating the territory of what was and was not acceptable as a child, especially when nuanced by culture, religion, and our closed-loop family system, was incredibly difficult. Add onto that my incessant desire for adult praise and you have a very early recipe for pain avoidance. As a result, I tried to read other people's emotions and thoughts through their body language, facial expressions, and what I now know today as intuition, all for the purpose of avoiding those unwanted punishments and feeling some amount of love and worth via praise.

Just a year after my great classroom disturbance the forming needs of avoidance solidified in a truly detrimental way. I was in the third grade and I'd had enough with the whole confession thing. For those of you who haven't had the experience, *confession*, at least in my Catholic grade school, was the weekly ritual of listing out your sins to a priest who would then give you a *penance* to make up for your *transgressions* (who knew what those words meant anyway). Every Wednesday we'd walk single-file across the courtyard to the church, wait our turn to sit in a stuffy, wooden box with the old priest, tell him how we had fought with our siblings and didn't do our homework, and then received our sentencing in the form of reciting numerous *Hail Marys* and dozens of *Our Fathers* as we kneeled back in the pews. I hated the weekly reminder that I was a piece of shit.

One day I had the bright idea to just avoid sin entirely by doing everything perfectly. *Duh!* The simplicity of it practically smacked me in the face so for an entire week I forced myself to do my homework on time, get the dishes done before mom even asked, and walked away (with much effort) from every potential fight over the Legos and *Star Wars* action figures. And let me tell you, I *did* do everything perfectly and when the next Wednesday rolled around I was beyond excited to go to confession! I imagined myself walking in, stating my triumph to the pathetic old man before being asked to return to the pew to *sit down* like the queen I knew myself to be instead of kneeling and praying like the rest of the peasants. The church would practically have to declare my sainthood on the spot. But after I confessed, the words that fell out of the priest's mouth were so far from what I had anticipated that I had to ask him to repeat himself. He said something to the effect of, "My child (they really do say that), you have committed a grievous sin, the sin of selfishness. In your desire to escape the justice of God your good intentions and actions were not truly for the benefit of others or even for God but for yourself to avoid punishment. This is a great sin." I was crushed. Not only did I feel completely defeated, but I was assigned what felt like a million *Acts of Contrition*, a most complicated prayer for a third grader. I was the last to finish praying and used the sleeve of my shirt to quietly soak up my tears at the back of the line. There was no winning, there was no way to be a good person, I was and always would be a sinner. So I turned to the only form of processing I knew and started keeping my sins a secret from even God, lying to the priest each week by confessing to a single fight or a single instance of forgotten homework which was only worth ten *Hail Marys* and I hated myself for it every time.

I'm not proud of saying this, but in learning how to keep all of those secrets my lying habit ballooned and when my lies started to pile up my family stopped believing me. One day, as I was pulling on the navy-blue checkered skirt I wore as part of my Catholic school uniform, I heard the unmistakable moo of a cow in the driveway just beneath my bedroom window. I froze, not quite sure I correctly placed the sound at first since we lived in the city and usually only heard cows when we drove through the empty expanses that permeated Iowa but that *must* have been a moo...

The whir of my mom's hair dryer exploded in the bathroom across the hall and jolted me back to the task at hand. I shook my head and finished tucking in my shirt before jogging down the hallway to the living room to gather my books for school. I skidded to a stop. Standing there in the big bay window looking directly at me was the biggest cow I had ever seen. My mouth dropped open a little and then dropped open even more as I saw she wasn't the only one. There were cows *everywhere*. They were all over our front hill eating the grass, pooping in the neighbor's yard, and walking down the middle of the street! It was *awesome*.

Questions flooded my mind as I remembered that there was a farmer at the end of our street and dad said once that he hadn't wanted to move when the city started building around him. He must have kept cows on the other side of his farm where we couldn't usually see and, somehow, they must have found a way out and through the fence that separated his land from the park on the corner. Remembering the park, I darted over to the playroom window and giggled with glee while jumping up and down at the sight of three cows on the jungle gym. This was almost as good as imagining that I was in one of my *Magic Tree House* books with Morgan LeFay.

I yelled for my mom to come see the *massive* herd of *giant* cows eating our grass but the hair dryer angrily picked up speed, whirring at an unfathomably high octave that plainly said she was ignoring me. I went back to the front window where the first cow was still peering through the glass and got close. People always said cows had brown eyes but these ones definitely looked black to me. She was beautiful and fascinating and huge. I couldn't take it anymore, mom *had* to see that there were cows in the front yard because one of them was looking right at me! I decided to risk it. I ran down the hall and threw the bathroom door open, reflexively grabbing the handle before it slammed into the wall, and quickly assessed the situation. I deemed it a dangerous one as she turned to glare at me with her groovy eye but this information was too important to let go and my brothers were downstairs playing, so I was the only one that knew the incredible truth: that there were cows in our yard right in front of the bay window. Big ones.

"Mom, there are COWS in the yard. COOOWS!" I said, drawing out the vowel to convey the gravity of the situation.

She huffed a curt sigh and slammed her comb down on the counter. *Not good.*

"Megan, you have to stop making things up! No one will ever believe you if you keep lying like this. Now go and pack your lunch because I'm not doing it for you!"

So there were limits to lying which meant there were limits to secrets too but how do you keep secrets without lying? That train of thought would have to wait for another time. Reassessing the situation I determined that I could still get her attention on this if I said it in the right way. I took a deep breath and brought out the most even, adult-sounding voice I could muster.

"Mom," I said, the perfect vision of her mini-me, "I'm telling the truth and you have to come look. There's a big one right in the front window."

Her eyes narrowed threateningly but she decided against explosive anger (just as I'd read she would) and with a sharp exhale of frustration she put down the dryer and picked up the hair spray, walking with me out the door in a mist of chemical-smelling death. *Worth it*, I thought as I held my breath to avoid choking on the fumes. As soon as she locked eyes with the cow outside the window she burst into laughter. *Double worth it.*

My brothers came scrambling upstairs after the danger was over and squealed with delight.

"Moo cows!" they yelled, climbing onto the bay window's edge. "Mooooooooo!"

Our mooing was short-lived as mom shushed us to call the farmer, finding his number in the big yellow phone book that sat at the end of the countertop. Her eyes twinkled as her fingers twirled the cord of the handset and she told the man that his cows were loose in the city.

"Mom!" I whispered excitedly, "Don't forget to tell him they're on the playground too!"

She shushed me again but smiled. The farmer came and collected his herd as we packed into the old Chevy Lumina on the way to school.

"Glad you were telling the truth this time, Meg-a-roni. Nobody likes a liar."

Noted.

I was running as fast as I could through the twisted trees of a foggy forest. They were right behind me—the witches—and they were catching up fast. I was too small, too short, and too young to outrun them. My lungs burned from the exertion and the smoke that choked the air.

With a quick glance back I saw that they had torches.

Everything started going up in flames. All of the trees were burning. The witches were coming. They were close and I couldn't outrun them.

They wanted to burn me alive.

(*Exploration and Interpretation, Chased by Witches*)

Several years ago now, when I was in my late twenties, I visited my hometown of Dubuque and went for a walk with my mom to "talk some things out." It was one of the last times I saw her in person and it's seared into my memory because it was the first time she openly acknowledged The Green Bean Incident. I was perhaps seven or eight years old when it happened and had been testing the boundaries of our household. One evening at dinner we were served green beans. I had always disliked green beans and refused to eat the serving on my plate.

"Megan," my mom scolded, "You won't get dessert if you don't eat those green beans."

"That's ok," I said. "I don't need dessert." (I really wanted to see where this would go.)

"Well you're not getting up from the table until you eat them," my dad sternly chipped in.

"That's ok," I said. "I already got my homework done and I don't mind sitting here." (It was a lie but I could be very stubborn.)

"Fine. Stay here then."

I did. I stayed there. For hours. It got dark outside and I stubbornly remained in my seat staring at the cold green beans and thinking I had won the argument. They'd have to drop me off at school in the morning so I only had... ten hours left. I could do that. I laid my head down on the table and started to doze off.

WHOOSH

My back hit the table and knocked the wind out of me. They'd come in fast, picking me up and slamming me down next to the green beans. Mom squeezed both of my arms, pinning them painfully at my sides while dad gripped my legs with his own. He reached over for the cold green beans and picked up a handful before shoving them into my mouth along with his fingers. He pushed them down, scraping the soft walls of my throat with his fingernails. I panicked and started thrashing, gagging on his fingers and the green beans as tears rolled down my cheeks. He kept going. I didn't know what was happening and the beans definitely weren't in small enough pieces to swallow but he continued to shove them down in handfuls anyway. I vomited. Dad yelled with disgust. Then he shoved another fistful of green beans down my throat with his fingers *and* my vomit. I felt my face burning from the lack of oxygen and thought back on the time I watched him almost beat Sasha to death. I prayed to God in my head and begged for my own life. They stopped before I passed out and I was allowed to live.

When I brought this up to my mom 20 years later she sucked some air into her mouth between her teeth and grimaced.

"Oooo," she said, narrowing her eyes with a pained look. "You remember that? That's too bad. I'd hoped you'd've forgotten."

My nightmares were not formed from their momentary traumatic roots alone, they were a product of the perfect storm, an amalgamation of the persistent environmental, experiential, and psychological circumstances that made up the bulk of my childhood. Built on a foundation of keeping secrets, telling lies to keep those secrets, and avoiding the truth of those secrets at all costs, the pain and hurt in my mind-body-energy system only grew. In later years, my mom would occasionally bring up memories, regaling tales of how destructive and emotionally explosive my siblings and I had been as kids. We'd laugh about the absurdity of it all, using humor as a coping mechanism, but part of me wondered if this was just her way of acknowledging that she knew something traumatic was happening to each of us even though it was difficult for her to admit it (let alone her own part in it).

One of the tales that strikes me the hardest depicts my first big "freak out session" (my mom's label for explosive behaviors and panic attacks). I was four years old and in the middle of a massive tantrum when my parents determined that they didn't know what to do with me. They decided to carry me into the little half bath across from the laundry room and lock me inside until I wore myself out. The confined, sterile room did nothing to soothe me and I proceeded to completely decimate the space including the ceramic pedestal sink which I promptly ripped clean off the wall in a hulked-out feat of rage. Again, I was four. While I don't have this memory myself, I've heard it recounted enough times to relay it with confidence and it gives me some modicum of comprehension for how much pain my mind-body-energy system was holding onto even then.

Eventually, the weight of all that pain and the secrets I had been keeping began to collapse inward, carving out a black well of heavy gravity where the love of my heart should have been, and sending me deep into the realm of deep depression. The more I experienced of life, the more my nightmares flourished and I began associating sleep with a form of torture. I was drowning in the complexity of my experiences. I didn't have the tools to help me out of it nor was I in an environment that was safe to open up and begin the healing process. Something was very, very wrong.

2
Why Can't Ice Cream Fix This?

I love ice cream. I have always loved it. Chocolate chip cookie dough is my classic go-to though today I've moved on to the very specific and far superior Culver's Butterfinger Concrete-Mixer. Custard is just better. I have fond memories of ice cream at almost every age but most of those memories end up taking me back to Mississippi Lock and Dam #11 just beneath Eagle Point Park. Every year for the Fourth of July we'd stuff our camping chairs into the trunk and drive downtown towards Sutton Pool (the one with the giant mushroom waterfall) to get the best seats for the city fireworks. We'd park as close as we could before joining the throngs of people all walking in the same direction. I loved the fireworks but I *really* loved stopping at the old-fashioned Dairy Queen for the largest sized chocolate chip cookie dough blizzard my parents would allow me to eat all summer. We each liked something different. My brother liked to get cherry dipped cones like mom (or the old cherry Mr. Freeze), our sibling Sasha liked the swirl cones and I think dad liked the brownie batter blizzard before he met a guy named Tony Robbins who convinced him to only eat leafy turtle food.

We're talking about ice cream because this is a book reviewing my life but also because shit's about to get real. So when you see the phrase "ice cream" throughout the rest of this chapter I want you to breathe and remember that I made it through this and I can still recall the wonder of those Fourth of July nights at the retro Dairy Queen and laugh about it too.

One day in the eighth grade I told my mom that I needed the family computer for an hour to write a report for school. It was a lie. I wasn't really writing a paper, I was looking for the sexually explicit fanfiction I had saved in a folder inside another folder and inside several more after that—the outlet of a young fantasy nerd trying to make sense of hormones, past sexual abuse, and good old-fashioned Catholic repression. While I was searching for my smut, I came across another set of folders that practically mirrored the intention of my own. My curiosity engaged at the prospect of uncovering someone else's secret so I started to dig. Eventually, I got to the bottom of the bottom of their folder system and clicked on a video that had an intentionally basic title. But as the video began to play my entire body tensed up and I knew that something was very, very wrong. There was a woman in the video sitting down and facing the camera but she wasn't using the chair properly and she was completely naked. She sat leaned back with her legs splayed open shoving something repeatedly into her privates. It reminded me of something I had seen before and as the realization of *that* memory surfaced, my face reddened with panic and shame and I froze. My whole body began shaking with intense fear and a blood-curdling scream sent shockwaves through my lungs as tears poured down my cheeks. Rushing upstairs to check on me, my mom saw what was on the screen and realized this was not something I had just come across on AOL instant messenger or Bebo (do you remember Bebo?), this was something that I had discovered in a file folder on the computer while snooping. This was someone else's. I was inconsolable as the tears streamed down my face. I couldn't hear anything, I couldn't feel anything, I couldn't see anything, all I could do was scream.

I spent the rest of the day curled up and shaking in my bed and when my dad got home from work that night my mom's screams filled the house, replacing mine. Maybe it's just the blur of trauma skewing my memory but in the weeks that followed my mom suddenly became kind and gentle, taking me for mother-daughter dates to get ice cream or to see a funny movie. Dad became pretty absent as he suddenly got busy at work and had to stay late every night for a "big project." But it didn't matter how much ice cream I ate (though the chocolate chip cookie dough *did* make me feel better momentarily) or how many funny movies we saw, I couldn't get that naked woman out of my head and I began to review what I had experienced as a kid.

It started with just observing the memories but then I started becoming aware of the gravity of those experiences and I found some comprehension for what, exactly, I had done to my brother all those years ago. We had talked about sexual assault briefly in school and I realized that's what I had done to him when I was six and he was four. And that was what had been done to me. I loathed myself.

To my recollection, neither of my parents really knew how to effectively address the event and my reaction to it so they just sort of let it drift away. I didn't want to bring it up either because if I did then they'd know one of my biggest secrets and *that* one could destroy my family so I made the decision to begin destroying myself instead. Every day after school I would come home and lay in bed for hours at a time as I walked around in my imagination. I started packing up my secrets in organized mental boxes and putting them away, hiding them in the basement of my memory. I imagined that I was in Middle-Earth with the fellowship and we were on a quest to burn all of my memories in the fiery pits of Mount Doom. I started physically hurting myself because somehow it felt right. I never cut my skin because I knew someone would see it and I needed to maintain my secrets so I started punching the tops of my legs until they bruised and biting my tongue until it bled. It felt good to punish myself, it felt right. At least, it felt like I was trying to make something right. But the guilt and self-loathing were becoming unbearable. I couldn't take it anymore.

Coming home from school one day I told my brothers they could watch as much TV as they wanted instead of doing the list of chores mom had left for us on the counter. As they scrambled off to the basement and settled into the den I went out to the garage and walked right over to the camping box. It was heavy but I managed to pull it down off the shelf and after a little rummaging I found exactly what I was looking for: the rope we would tie between two trees to hang our swimsuits and towels on.

That day at school I'd been daydreaming about an old Western I'd seen my grandma Judy watching on the small TV in her kitchen. In the movie, they made the bad guys hang for the crimes they committed and even though I didn't know how to make a noose, I knew you could die by hanging. It was the only way I could think of to end it all. I grabbed my backpack and emptied my textbooks onto the table to make space for the rope before heading out into the woods behind our house.

It's at this point that my memory gets a little blurry. I know that something happened to me out there but when my consciousness picked up again, I was sitting next to my brothers on the couch downstairs watching a show and laughing with them like I'd been there the whole time. I had no memory of walking home and getting the rope. I had no recollection of school that day. I had no idea why I even wanted to take that rope in the first place. The only thing I had was a sudden patchwork of empty spaces across the timeline of my life—whole years wiped out in an instant—but I felt better so I thought nothing of it.

Sometimes, you have to forget yourself to keep living for a while and that's ok. You'll find yourself again when you're ready to hold all of you.

The change in me was noticeable and while I didn't recall exactly what had happened or why I was so angry and hurt all the time, my mom saw it. I started randomly erupting in extreme emotional fits of agonized weeping, scream-crying, and bodily harm that mimicked the now seemingly easy-going "freak out sessions" I'd experienced as a younger kid. She tried to talk to me about it in her own way but by the time she acknowledged that something really was wrong, I wasn't myself anymore. In a last-ditch effort to figure out why I had become the way that I was, mom asked around and found a therapist despite my dad's insistence that shrinks were just conniving thieves that preyed on pathetically weak-minded people. I cried and begged my mom to turn the car around the whole way there, only shutting up when we entered the parking lot because I knew I'd suffer more if I made a scene in public.

The therapist's waiting room was dead silent, the kind where you can hear your own heart tripping in your chest. *What would the therapist do to me?* I wondered. *What punishment was I in for now?* No one had bothered to explain to me why I was here, what a therapist actually was, or that this *wasn't* a punishment. I don't think my mom even knew how to start the conversation and I certainly didn't know she was trying to help me.

The therapist called my name with a gentle smile and walked me down the long, dark tunnel to her office. Her line of questioning confused me at first. *Why is she asking me about how I feel in school and at home? What does she mean, 'do I feel safe'?* But then I saw through her charade. This was all an idea to get me to confess the secrets I had retained and that I was honor-bound to keep. I didn't even know what the secrets were anymore but I knew that this woman was hired to wrangle them out of me and I knew that I might die if she tried.

As she prodded deeper with her line of questions, a series of memories flashed unbidden through my mind:

I'm clutching a book bag to my chest as I sit in the woods behind our house, snow falling gently in the night. It's stuffed with clothes and peanut butter and jelly sandwiches. But I can't do it. I can't run away and live like the Boxcar children. I feel so stupid as I sneak back inside.

*

I'm screaming, threatening to call the child-protection services I just learned about in school as my brother cowers on the floor crying with big red handprints all over him. My dad's eyes widen and I feel powerful. But that power is short-lived as mom physically drags me into the minivan and clicks the child locks behind me. She gets in the driver's seat and starts screaming into the void of the night, screaming at me, screaming at dad, screaming at her life, screaming at everything. I think about trying to comfort her but I'm shaking in the vice grip of debilitating despair just trying to keep myself in one piece. She drives me to a building called Hillcrest and pulls over to make sure I can see it.

"This is where kids go when their families can't handle them anymore," she says, her voice dripping with venom. "They lock them up and take them away from their siblings forever. They watch your every move as you sleep and eat and shit until they kick you out onto the streets at eighteen. Is this where you want to go? Because if it is, I'll walk you in there right now and you'll never see any of us again."

I get on my knees in the back of the minivan and beg.

*

"You came outta me!" mom laughs, using her My Cousin Vinny voice. I had just mentioned something about going away for college but now I get the sense that I'm supposed to stay here. The phrase is her way of reminding us of the debt we owe her for existing. She gave up her life for us—her dreams. She could have been an architect, but she had to become a nurse and marry dad and give birth to us instead.

"Who's gonna take care of me when I'm old?!" she mocks.

We always laugh when she says it like that. It's supposed to be funny. *But then why does it feel so wrong?* I ask myself.

*

I'm in the upstairs bathroom when time slows down. My right hand reaches back, fingers splaying out wide, as I move to smack my mom as hard as I can across her face.

I don't want to do it. Really, I don't. But she's so angry right now that she's becoming someone else. Her face doesn't look quite right, her eyes have literally gone black with anger, pupils dialed at 100% like she's possessed by the devil, and she's screaming, mouth open wide, less than an inch from my face. But the most terrifying thing is that no words are coming from her vocal chords, she's just screaming the color black.

A vision flashes into my mind coupled with the power of energetic gravity—she's grabbing my head and smashing it into the sink. A knowing terror fills my stomach. She actually might do that. I don't want to die this way. I don't want her to have to be the one to do it. I want my mom back.

I don't even think about it. It's pure survival instinct as I slap her with everything I have.

WHACK!

It works.

Both of us stand still, shocked into silence, until the 'I'm-so-sorries' pour out of my mouth at a million miles an hour, but it doesn't matter, her response bears finality.

"Sorry isn't good enough."

I don't deserve a bedroom door now, dad removes it from the hinges after he gets done hitting me. I'm lower than low, less than the significance of an earthworm. The handprints are starting to fade but the door doesn't come back for some time. They're always watching me, like I think those people do at Hillcrest.

The therapist's office (*the shrink's office*, I sneered) snapped back into focus and I vowed that she'd never get a confession out of me. My parents were perfect, as most parents are, and I did love them (truly, I did), but no one could take the secrets away from me. So I lied my ass off.

"What about home?" she asked, again. "Your mom mentioned that she's worried about you and the descriptions of these emotional episodes tell me she's onto something. Do you feel safe at home?"

"Yes, ma'am," I said with the perfect lilt to support my lie. I'd been studying this woman since she came to get me in the waiting room and I felt like I understood her angle. "I feel perfectly safe at home, but..." I paused for dramatic effect and mustered the most pitiful look of sorrow and concern that I could, lowering my voice to a calculated hush. "I think my mom's just using me as an excuse to talk to you. My parents have been fighting and my mom cries a lot, kind of like what she says I do. I'm really worried about her but please, please don't tell her I said that because I'll get in trouble for telling you. She says she can handle it. You see, my dad says you're a shrink and we can't go see shrinks because they're a waste of money."

I knew exactly what I was doing and though I'm pretty sure she saw right through me, she also knew this lie was partly a truth. She thanked me for my honesty (my stomach sank with guilt but

I knew I did what had to be done) and took me back out to the waiting room. My mom looked up with a bit of suspicion, it hadn't been that long, but the therapist had a convincing smile and asked for me to take a seat up front while she took my mom back instead, "to talk about Megan." They stayed back there for the whole rest of the appointment and when she came out, I saw the dried-up riverbeds of tears on my mom's cheeks. There was no ice cream to get today. We drove home in silence and never went back.

The rest of the year passed quickly and because we moved, I soon found myself at a different high school than all of my junior high friends. This turned out to be a blessing and I thrived in a new environment where I could redefine who I was without anyone knowing who I had been before. I formed many close friendships and as soon as I got a job and a driver's license I spent as much time with them as possible.

We were a mix of choir and band nerds who loved *The Lord of the Rings*, *Star Wars*, and everything *Harry Potter* (which was still releasing books at the time). We met up at the midnight releases for *Half-Blood Prince* and *The Deathly Hallows* fully dressed in wizard garb and ready to read the shit out of whatever magick lay in those pages. Being a nerd was hard sometimes because most of us were single and while we all had crushes on each other, no one seemed to have the balls to ever really do anything about it which resulted in many trips to Walmart for Lonely People Ice Cream.

Lonely People Ice Cream was both an activity and a statement. We would declare the date and time after theater practice and meet up in the Walmart parking lot before storming the freezer section in search of the latest flavors of Ben & Jerry's mini cups. After walking through the register one by one (I apologize if you were an employee at the Dubuque Walmart back then and remember us) we'd swarm out to our cars and eat our ice cream while bemoaning our collective single-ness and gossiping about who touched a boob in a closed practice room when they were supposed to be playing the tuba. The freedom to get ice cream with my friends whenever I wanted was awesome but it never could quite drown out the feeling that something was still very wrong.

As my high school years passed I could feel a dissonance growing between myself and pretty much everything in my environment. I hated going home at the end of the day and I hated the endless list of chores that I was expected to delegate to my siblings and ensure the completion of before mom got home. With the gaps in my memory I had almost entirely forgotten about what I had done to my brother when we were kids and the knowledge of where my actions had been learned wholly disappeared. I lived half of the time as the new version of my high school persona and half of the time as a walking nightmare that emotionally exploded without warning. I was an A's and B's honors student who took AP courses for the advanced college credit but got grounded from my junior prom because I punched my brother in the face when he said something nasty. I sang in four different choirs, made all-state as an alto, and even performed in Carnegie Hall, New York with the North American Honors Choir all the while imagining myself walking down the street with a billowing black cloak that spilled gallon after gallon of self-hatred and loathing upon the sidewalk at my feet.

I thought about going to college out of state or at least outside of Dubuque. My mom yo-yoed back and forth between supporting me in moving and trying to convince me to stay but she took me to tour some colleges anyways. We first went to Madison but I didn't want to live in Wisconsin. Then we traveled to Iowa City to check out the University of Iowa but it was too overwhelming for me. We went to Decorah to investigate Luther College—they had an amazing music program—and while I loved the feel of it, I felt like something I was looking for was missing. I even went up to Minneapolis (my current home) to look into the University of Minnesota but, like Luther, it felt like it was missing something. In the end I graduated high school and spent the summer working two jobs in preparation for Loras College, my parents' alma mater, where I'd begrudgingly signed up for classes because I couldn't afford to leave town.

My first semester went horribly. I barely passed my courses and kept feeling an intense urge to escape and leave everything behind. I knew that something was definitely, incredibly wrong. That January, my parents asked me to stay home one evening and sat us all in the living room to announce that they were getting a divorce. My eyes burned as I promptly got up and left without saying a word.

I had failed. All of the secrets I had kept, all the lies I had told, had been for nothing. We were *not* a perfect family, my childhood had been a sham, and if we weren't perfect then that meant I had to look at my own imperfections as well.

3

Oo-Fuckin'-Rah

Recruits all over the country join the military for a myriad of reasons. Some recruits want a steady paycheck, some want the GI Bill for a college degree, and some are military brats and want to carry on their family tradition, but at the end of the day all recruits join to serve their country. Some rendition of that always fell from my lips when people asked me why, in God's name, I was giving my life up to Uncle Sam. These same people also lacked the faith that I could actually make it through boot camp. Little did they know that I had already spent my whole life in a boot camp of sorts. "I want to serve my country," was just one more pseudo-lie that was maybe a little bit true too.

I remember, like so many people, exactly where I was when the first plane hit the Twin Towers on 9/11: Mrs. Casey's class, third floor of the New Building, Language Arts, 5th grade. Another teacher rushed in and told her to turn on the TV and we all knew something was terribly wrong when she started crying but we were sent home before we could ask much about it. We didn't have cable at home, so mom took us over to grandpa's house where we sat on the floor in the living room watching the towers crumble and listening to the trembling voices of the adults in the kitchen. The memory of that day sat at the forefront of my mind as I made my decision to enlist. I knew I absolutely wanted to do something to better the world. I wanted to fight for what I believed in. I wanted to find a purpose. But Freedom and Country climbed into the back seat when good old Escape-the-Fuckery demanded to get behind the wheel. What I really needed was to get out of Iowa.

College wasn't working out for me and after the news of my parents' impending divorce I failed several classes my second semester—the first time I had ever academically failed anything. I avoided telling my family for as long as possible and started taking regular breaks to go cry in my car for seemingly no reason at all but one thing I clearly knew was that I needed to leave the state and possibly even the country. A-S-A-P. I didn't know what to do, where to go, or how to even get started so I did what I always did when life got really, really difficult and fell into a series of daydreams at work. At that point in time, I was blessed with a non-social job deep in the bowels of the local acute care center where I worked as a medical records clerk. The tasks were easy and the work was relatively solitary so I gave myself a present: five days to daydream different scenarios or locations I might escape to!

For a whole week after clocking in, I'd plug my headphones into an iPod nano, collect the massive binders of patient charts in a small wire shopping cart (in the days before online chart systems there were physical binders containing your medical history—some people had several massive binders chock full of their records), filed them away like a wannabe librarian, and asked the universe what in the world I was going to do. In one daydream I was joining the peace corps and went to El Salvador to build houses. In another, I sold my car and all my possessions, bought a one-way plane ticket to Europe, and backpacked through the Alps before meeting the love of my life and working in a cafe. But on Friday my daydreams led me to the military and I suddenly found myself in a hyper-realistic, very visual hellscape.

It was like I had been interjected into a movie. Without warning, I was just *there*, jumping out of a boat that was pushing towards a sandy shoreline, gunfire, and heavy artillery from the forts up the hill blasting all around me. I looked left and right and saw the faces of men that I knew were in my squad (somehow I just *knew* them). We felt the keel rub across a sandbar and leapt out into the fray. I screamed as we charged towards the shore, pulsing with adrenaline and barely contained terror, forcing my legs to push through water that was growing redder every second with the swirling rivulets of blood and chunks of flesh that had been blown off of our mates in the other boats. It was the energy of chaos. We didn't get far before I watched, wide-eyed, as one of my friends took several bullets to the chest and collapsed beneath the rusty-brown surface, drowning before he could bleed out. Eventually, half of us made it to the beach and into the semi-safety of the dunes before sunset. The smells of bloody sweat, shit, and an open tin of what looked like canned beef in my hands easily prevented any form of sleep that night... (Many years later I would identify this memory that wasn't a memory as the Battle of Gallipoli from WWI). The whole scenario felt like I'd dreamt it before, like I'd *lived* it before, and in that moment, somehow, I knew I wanted to do it—the military. I wanted to do it because I knew I'd already done it.

I dropped a chart on my foot and snapped out of the daydream, shaking it off as a weird (very, very weird) hyper-imaginative bit of escapism. My shift ended shortly after and I wrapped the headphone cord back around my iPod nano before clocking out and driving home.

The minute I walked into my mom's house the landline rang, jerking me out of the last bits of my military reverie.

"Shit!" I hissed (that word would soon be replaced with the Marine Corp's favorite word, "fuck").

Uncharacteristically, and with a sort of magnetic pull I ran upstairs to grab the phone off the wall.

"Niemer residence," I said, gritting my teeth.

"Hello there, this is Marine Corps Recruiter Sergeant Moreno. Is Megan available?"

"...This is she," I slowly replied, looking around for the green lines of code that would tell me if I were in the *Matrix*.

"Oh! Good to get a hold of you! We were just looking back at our local high school survey records and noticed that you showed interest in the military a couple of years ago. I'd love to talk to you about enlisting if it's something you're still interested in?"

Was this really happening right now? I was just getting blown to bits with the friends in my head and less than an hour later this dude was asking me if I *actually* wanted to get blown to bits... What were the odds?

"Uh... yeah, sure," I replied.

"Great. When might you be available to come down for a chat?"

"Well," I wracked my brain for an excuse but couldn't find one, "to be honest, I'm free right now."

There was a brief pause on the other end of the line as the Sergeant was likewise processing this incredibly fruitful and perhaps divinely timed phone call.

"Yeah, I can do now!" he blurted out.

After providing me with directions to the recruiting center we hung up and I got right back in the car, throwing a sweatshirt over my work uniform before driving off to meet my destiny.

A couple of months later, in November of 2011, I signed the dotted line and enlisted. I had needed to lose some weight and work myself down to an acceptable 1.5-mile run time which Sergeant Moreno selflessly helped me with (though, years later, I learned that there's sometimes a monetary incentive for recruiters to get women to enlist). I was ready for boot camp.

At the time, the Marine Corps was the only branch of the military that completely separated their recruits by gender for boot camp. I marched with women, went to class with women, and lived every moment surrounded only by women. While the experience of gendered boot camp can build foundations of sexism and foster narratives of gender inequality in the fleet (an issue the Marine Corps is currently grappling with at the time of this writing), I honestly appreciated it. We were a platoon of badass women learning from badass women Marines and there was an unspoken understanding between all of us.

For three months I learned all about the Halls of Montezuma and the shores of Tripoli, how to walk in an echelon formation, never to leave my weapon unattended, how to shoot that weapon well, how to maintain discipline under pressure, and that my frizzy curls could lay flat if I used enough gel. Every morning before reveille the Hair Fairy came to visit those with locks below their neckline. She disguised herself as the recruit assigned to the night's last watch and encouraged the owners of long hair to get their shit-up-in-a-bun before LIGHTS or we'd all pay the price. Even though we were surrounded by the color green, this wasn't Oz and Glinda's magick had nothing on us. Fuck yeah. Bitchin'.

(As a note, swearing is an integral component of military vernacular rooted in the physically, psychologically, and emotionally difficult moments all members of the armed forces experience in one way or another. Today, science shows us that curse words activate the body's "fight or flight" response and can trigger the production of adrenaline which results in a natural form of pain relief. It is for this reason that the amount of swearing in this book is about to increase—it has become a part of my everyday narrative.)

But boot camp wasn't all OORAHs and moto-runs. Reality was ever-present and our platoon experienced more difficulty than most, kicking off our *real* journey at the end of our first week when we were suddenly woken in the middle of the night by the searing brightness of the overhead lights.

"EVERYONE SHOVE YOUR FACES UNDER YOUR PILLOWS!" a drill instructor yelled with the tiniest vocal waver.

This was not a typical wake up call for LIGHTS (the Hair Fairy *always* came first). No, this was different. It was still pitch black outside and there were male voices near the door of our squad bay (the male recruits were kept on the other side of Parris Island so this was really, really weird). I peaked out from under my pillow and saw four EMTs wheeling a stretcher past my rack and into the head (a Navy term for bathroom). A few minutes later they came back out with a cloth draped over the figure of a fellow recruit who was strapped to the stretcher. *Holy fuck*, I thought. *Is she dead?*

"There's a man with a camera coming in here," the drill instructor called. "He needs to take photos for the investigation. KEEP YOUR FACES COVERED! Under NO circumstances will your faces be photographed!"

Too late, she saw me peeking and stood up on my footlocker to physically shove my head into the mattress.

"DO NOT SHOW YOUR FACE!" she screamed directly into my ear.

I had no idea what was happening but I knew it wasn't good. We learned in the morning that the recruit had attempted suicide but, thankfully, had lived. The photos were to document anything needed for the investigation and it would move faster (and be more beneficial for the recruit) if the rest of our platoon's identities remained anonymous. She had tried to hang herself by her bootlaces from the bars across the toilet stalls. Something twisted in the pit of my stomach when we were given that information but I couldn't quite place it.

We banded together a little differently for recruits after that, not only bonding through the typical trials that only the Marine Corps could have put us through but by keeping each other psychologically and spiritually alive as well. We checked in with our rackmates regularly during free hour, tried to talk sense into the blue falcons (also known as "buddy-fuckers" or slackers—they brought down collective punishment), and late at night when we pretended to be sleeping we'd hug our sisters and make sure they were writing home to their families and loved ones for support.

I've never been particularly athletic but I have always been resilient and capable of mentally pushing myself past every seemingly impossible hurdle. I got the ever-loving shit IT'd (Intensive Training) out of me more than most in my platoon and was pulled into every sand pit on the island to push my body and mind past every imaginable limit again and again. Boot camp wasn't just insanely intense though, we did have *some* fun and we learned that the drill instructors did have a sense of humor, they just weren't allowed to be seen laughing. When they couldn't contain themselves, they'd take their campaign covers off and hold them over their faces until they regained composure. Part of their banter lay in the nicknames they bestowed upon certain recruits which was more a mark of honor than a form of humiliation. They gave me two nicknames, Teen Wolf and Sasquatch, for the sideburns that grew down my cheeks and below my jaw as a result of my PCOS (Polycystic Ovarian Syndrome)—we weren't allowed to use razors for the first two months.

I hated the nicknames before I understood that they weren't strictly meant as insults so when we were allowed to finally shave I wiped the sideburns clean off my face without hesitation. Of course, there are no secrets in boot camp and I was quickly swarmed by the drill instructors the next morning. It was the look in Sergeant Cortez' eyes, a momentary mix of compassion and gentleness, that clued me into the true intent of my nicknames and on the way out for PT (Physical Training) she said, "That's too bad, Niemer, now you look like everyone else. How're we going to know it's you in formation? You blend in again." Something about the way she said it told me that I didn't need to be ashamed of my natural body hair. I let my sideburns grow out after that.

As the weeks carried on we dropped more recruits to routine injuries, though thankfully nothing self-inflicted like the recruit who was wheeled out of the squad bay in our first week. Besides that, Marine Corps boot camp was everything you'd expect it to be: challenging, chaotic, and life-changing. Weirdly, I loved it.

Then, just as soon as it had seemingly begun, three months had passed and it was all over. I spent thirty minutes roaming the floor at graduation searching for my parents who hadn't recognized me twenty-five pounds lighter and when we finally reunited, I bathed in their pride (which I still equated to love) for only a moment before the awkwardness set in and I remembered that they were still divorced and all this pleasantness was just a charade for the people around us. Our family system of secrets was still trying to figure this one out.

At one point, my dad convinced us to take a walk through the parking lot and revealed that he had rented a shiny new Mustang convertible. I had never cared about cars nor shown an interest in them but he really wanted to show it off. Something clicked and I understood that the Mustang had nothing to do with me and my graduation day, it was there to show my mom what she was missing. He even went so far as to ask her to take a photo of him and I posing in front of it because he was just so proud that I was a Marine and it would be a cool photo for me in my uniform with the Mustang that I didn't care for. I forced the smile to stay fixed on my face but knew that me and my achievements were still nothing more than props.

After basic training we were allowed to go home for a week before continuing on to MCT (Marine Combat Training) but my excitement to return to Iowa quickly dissipated when I walked in the front door of my mom's house and immediately felt like a stranger (dad had moved out and into the apartment above his parents' house). I was proud of what I had achieved and finally felt some sense of being grounded in my life, but everyone looked at me with pity and awkwardness, unable to comprehend why I had chosen to not only join the military but enlist in the most intense branch there was (though we Marines would say the *best* branch). There was no winning here. Everyone suddenly had opinions of my life choices and made sure to vocalize them. My cousin told me I looked sickly skinny, my old coworkers asked me when I'd be done and moving back to Dubuque to settle down and have kids, my friends said they felt like they didn't know me anymore and my mom kept staring hauntingly at my body and reminiscing about the days when she was in track and field because apparently the weight-loss made me look just like her now.

But my soul cried out the hardest when one of my best friends said, "I didn't actually think you'd make it through. What are you going to do now?"

"Be a Marine," I said, hardening my gaze as I wondered if any of these people had ever really known me at all. (A better question would have been "Had I ever felt safe enough to *let* them know me at all?" but I'd figure that out soon enough.) It hurt that the only person who seemed truly proud of me was myself. I couldn't wait to leave and get back in my uniform.

The month I spent in MCT was intense but I made it through and bonded with the women in my new platoon quickly. After that I traveled to Corry Station in Pensacola, Florida to begin training for my initial MOS as a 2651, an intelligence systems engineer. I had scored high on my placement test thanks to all those honors and AP courses in high school and before leaving for boot camp I was awarded the opportunity to choose my job instead of being randomly assigned to one. I wanted to be like one of the side characters in a James Bond movie who handled all the new tech but I quickly realized that's not what this job was about. As my classes got underway I found myself struggling again like I had in my first year of college. I was grappling with the material and even though I carried flashcards with me everywhere and studied with friends outside of class I wasn't getting any better. My brain just couldn't wrap around the vocabulary of the job. I was great at the practical application exercises which meant I could do the work but I failed the written tests over and over again which were a necessary part of the position where I needed to be able to fluently explain to officers or other high-ranking individuals exactly what I was doing. Even though I could physically and mentally do the work, I'd be useless if I couldn't communicate it properly to my superiors. I failed my third test and was re-classed as a 2621, a signals analyst. Thankfully, I caught onto my new MOS well, grasping the material quickly, and settled into the rhythm of school.

I was stationed in Pensacola longer than most Marines because I had failed my initial MOS training but that wasn't necessarily a bad thing. I understood the ins and outs of our day-to-day routine well and became not only our platoon scribe (the note taker and coordinator) but assisted the platoon Sergeant by marching our Marines to class. I *loved* moving an entire column of Marines from one end of the base to the other. Not only did it require me to be loud as fuck so that I could be heard over the sound of marching boots but I was allowed to create my own ditties and tunes. I made it a game to see if I could get anyone to break down in laughter once we arrived and broke formation in front of the SCIF (Sensitive Compartmentalized Information Facility). I called cadence to the tunes of Darth Vader's *Imperial March*, the *Addams Family*, *Indiana Jones*, and a whole variety of nerdy, ridiculous songs that had never before been used to march a platoon of Marines across the parade deck.

It was in this facet, as the marching stand-in for our platoon Sergeant, that I faced my first real encounter with blatant sexism. A new Marine Captain had arrived to take over command of our battalion and one of his first decrees was that we'd all be dressing up in our khaki and green service uniforms on Fridays. Women Marines are issued both skirts and pants with their service and dress uniforms to honor the original attire of the sisters who came before us if we so choose. But instead of allowing us the choice to *choose* to honor our OG sisters, the captain directly ordered that the women *must* wear their skirts with pumps instead of pants and there's a rule (for good reason) that anyone wearing heels isn't allowed to march in formation. This was a problem because I was the person who marched our formation and I was no longer allowed to do so on Fridays by the imposed limits of my assigned uniform.

I was infuriated and only had a day to train a man to do what I had been doing for months. I *did* get my replacement up to speed but that Friday our formation was clunky and unconfident as he forgot some of the commands while under pressure. The whole while, as our male counterparts marched to class, the handful of women who were part of our platoon walked behind the formation in a gaggle as our heels clicked out-of-time on the pavement. Our platoon's lack of professionalism was verbally noted by the other services present. So when we arrived at the SCIF and broke formation to complete our morning duties it was with frustrated anger that I climbed the stairs to the staff room for the day's notes and directives from our platoon Sergeant. He took one look at me and already knew how I felt about it but asked if I wanted to speak my mind in an official capacity (and in a room full of other higher-ranking staff members of various branches).

"Yes, I would," I stated curtly. "Permission to speak freely, Sergeant?"

"Permission granted."

I unloaded. Calculating my words but not holding back an ounce of the rage that coursed through my veins, I expressed exactly how I felt about not having a choice to wear the skirt. Not only was I not being treated as an equal to the men around me but our entire platoon was suffering in my absence, having been reprimanded for our poor formational performance on the quarterdeck. It wasn't the Marine's fault who marched us that day, it was the lack of time to prepare and the complete ignorance of our Captain to the needs of our platoon. Somewhere in there I stated that, "...as a *Marine*, I deserve to march next to my brothers if I so choose." And by the end of my monologue, I was so fired up that I physically shook with ire.

The room fell silent as not only my leaders had stopped to listen but the Navy Chiefs and Air Force Tech Sergeants of our joint-command had paused to look around the corners of their cubicles as well. The Sergeant cleared his throat.

"Thank you for your honest opinion, Lance Corporal Niemer," he said. "I'll speak to the Captain and see what I can do."

I was back marching our platoon in my service pants the next Friday with half of our women marching in the ranks and the other half following behind after choosing to wear their skirts, as it should be.

Being a woman Marine takes 110% of everything you have. There's an added pressure to be better, faster, stronger, and smarter than the men around you. I constantly found myself having to prove my worth again and again. Running was the bane of my existence and I barely passed our 3-mile run times so I turned to proving myself with strength and smarts, sometimes lifting my two-hundred pound male friends into a fireman's carry and squatting them in the middle of the quad just because I could (and because they asked). Was it stupid? Absolutely. Was it necessary? If I wanted to maintain the just-out-of-childhood respect of my peers, yes.

As the months I spent in Pensacola dragged on, my nightmares suddenly returned. I'd forgotten about them, realizing that they'd disappeared that first night in boot camp and, in hindsight, knowing the stress that I was under as my mind and body were completely reshaped into Marine-material, it made sense. There just hadn't been enough capacity for me to dream through the intensity of it all but now that I was settling into a new routine the nightmares came crawling back.

I had my first real episode of sleep paralysis in my barracks room. I had woken up to the feeling of a terrifying presence in the space with me and looked around the barely-lit darkness for its source. There, in the corner of the ceiling, was a demonic figure not unlike the ghouls that roamed the halls in my childhood. It clung to the walls like an oversized spider and extended a long, forked, snake-like tongue that dripped with black venom to taste my fear. I tried to scream but nothing came out. My body was locked in a vice grip and I struggled to move so much as a finger. Then, I woke up for the second time, and the demon vanished. I sat up in bed and immediately turned on every light that I could. My roommate was missing as usual (probably having snuck off to her boyfriend's room again) so I pulled all of the pillows I could find onto my bed and sat wide awake in the comfort of my makeshift fort until morning. (Many years later I'd learn that sleep paralysis was often paired with false awakenings, a term used to describe the feeling of waking up in your room without actually having woken, only to then wake up *for real* on the second try.) On some level, I knew that even though I had escaped the nightmare I had been living, I hadn't escaped the nightmares themselves. They were a part of me, and I was going to need to face them sooner or later. I opted for later.

(*Exploration and Interpretation, Sleep Paralysis*)

My new Marine friends and I became close, sharing our life's experiences, connecting on a deeper level, and learning about life from areas all over the country. It was through them that I learned some of the stories I found myself telling about my childhood were actually vivid descriptions of physical and psychological abuse. At first I vehemently denied this, feeling the defensive mechanism of my family system rising up (*what was I doing sharing information I had been taught to keep a secret?!*), but they asked what I'd think if they told me what I had just told them and the obvious answer reared its ugly head. What was once the humor of a necessary coping mechanism was now an extra soggy Band-Aid waiting to be ripped off.

One of the friends I connected with the most was Cannon, an ex-Mormon who had gone bald at just twelve years old and who never missed an opportunity to joke about his shiny dome or make fun of religious absurdities. I don't recall if I ever told him about the nightmares but he knew I had trouble sleeping and every once in a while he'd sneak into my room while my roommate was with her boyfriend and sit with me until I fell asleep. There was nothing sexual between us, just a deep bond of friendship that I was eternally grateful for and when I woke in the morning he'd be gone but the magick of his presence always did its job and gifted me a night of peace.

As my A-school pressed on I continued stumbling along the path of self-identification and began to separate my innate sense of self from the identity my family had designed for me, finally unearthing a personality that was all my own. I started letting my parents' phone calls go to voicemail, eventually only speaking with them once or twice a month which then faded to once or twice a year. I spoke with my siblings even less, not quite sure how to grapple with the knowledge of how much I knew that I'd hurt them all, but the silence with my family, as well as the space to become my own person and step into a life of my own choosing, began to work. I felt something akin to hope and happiness bubble up under the surface though it was always mixed with an underlying sense of guilt and unworthiness.

After passing our exams, my class received the incredibly last-minute news that we would be sent to a new follow-on school at Goodfellow AFB in San Angelo, Texas instead of heading straight to the fleet like our predecessors. We were the first class to go through this schooling right after our training period at Corry Station and it couldn't have come at a worse time for my friend Cannon. It was Tuesday when they told us and he was supposed to be flying home to marry his high school sweetheart on Friday. As our Staff Sergeant broke the news, knowing full well that Cannon's wedding would have to be canceled, we received our first encounter with *the needs of the Marine Corps*. My heart ached for my friend as our squadmates Hoffman and Wolff physically restrained him from tackling our platoon sergeant. The needs of the Marine Corps always came first.

Personally, I enjoyed San Angelo. The four of us—Cannon, Hoffman, Wolff, and I—spent our first month maintaining fitness and taking online courses as we waited for other classes to graduate from Corry Station. In Pensacola, we'd been training in a joint-command environment which meant our classes had consisted of not only Marines but individuals from every other branch of the military as well. Here at Goodfellow, however, our classes would consist solely of Marines, hence the need for more Marine graduates to accumulate before we had a class big enough to start the program. The two months it took were pretty chill, all things considered, and it gave Cannon time to not only cool off (sort of) but his fiancé ended up coming to Texas for a small impromptu wedding which they'd follow with a more traditional one later.

Our fireteam grew closer during our extended time in Texas and we fully embraced the opportunity to sign out for the weekend and go camping off base, packing survival equipment into our vehicles and taking off into the wilderness. The funny thing about Texas is that livestock are sometimes allowed to graze all over BLM land (Bureau of Land Management), kind of like a free-for-all. There were mornings we'd wake up in the middle of a herd of cows which always brought back the memory of my encounter with that black-eyed heifer as she'd stared at me through the big bay window while my mom's hair dryer revved like a hurricane.

One morning, instead of the cows, we woke up surrounded by a blanket of thick fog. It had drizzled all night and soaked through the kindling we'd saved for the morning. The boys had all but given up on the big breakfast we planned to cook over a fire. Thankfully, I had a few tricks up my sleeve rooted in survival knowledge I'd picked up in the Boundary Waters of Minnesota when I was sixteen having spent three months at the Girl Scout canoe base in Ely training as a backcountry guide. I knew how to build a fire in any condition. Determination set, I took off to look for any remotely dry kindling lying under the small canopies of bushes, trees, and heavy clumps of brush. Returning with loaded arms I poked our fire stick into the remnants of last night's blaze and found the still-hot coals at the bottom that I was looking for. Creating a proper channel for the flow of air, I stacked the semi-dry kindling I'd found around the coals and breathed like a dragon until flames licked the moisture clear and a fire roared in the pit once again. I hadn't even used a match. I didn't need to see their gaping mouths or smell the sizzling fat of the bacon to know that I had once again earned their respect.

Sometime around that weekend, I started spending more time with Wolff. Not only was I turning into a sexually frustrated twenty-year-old but I had recently put an end to a fling I'd had in Pensacola with a boy I'd gotten handsy with but not much else (there were rules in military schooling environments to try and prevent sexual relationships and I was a big rule follower). I was terrified of committing long-distance to someone I'd only really known for a couple of weeks so I broke it off quickly when I arrived in Texas and before my heart felt any weirder than it already did. I'm not sure if that's what Wolff was waiting for or if it was completely spontaneous but eventually, we found ourselves at a small concert in the middle of a wheat field. He pulled me aside and asked if I wanted to slip away and go catch some shooting stars. Stargazing was one of our favorite things to do when we went camping as a group so I said yes without hesitation. He grabbed a blanket from the back of his Jeep and we hiked out into the dark fields far beyond the concert grounds. We talked for a while, looked up at the stars, and began a philosophical discussion. As much as I wish I could remember what we talked about, the only thing that mattered at the time was finally feeling his lips pressing against my own and the sex that followed. I lost my virginity surrounded by stars and under the gentle light of the moon.

Wolff became Isaac overnight and our relationship would become a foundational experience in my life's story but I knew we weren't meant for each other almost as soon as we began to try to be. Within the first week of our relationship, we found ourselves sitting in his Jeep after class in the middle of an argument about how I was spending time in the company of other men—men who were my friends. I immediately identified his possessiveness driven by jealousy, crossed my arms, and reminded him that I was a female Marine, a blip of a statistic in a male-dominated environment, and that practically *all* of my friends were men and I would continue to have friends that were men. I told him he'd just have to get over it. He balled up his fists, screamed into the void just like my mom had all those years ago, and punched the ever-loving fuck out of his vehicle's console for a solid minute. Shock coursed through my body. I had never seen someone lose their shit so violently... except when I was a kid. And as much as I knew that I needed to end it right then and there, I simply couldn't. He was hurting from something just as much as I was and my heart wouldn't let him go.

The course carried on and we graduated from our last class (this time it really was the last one), receiving the assignments for our first duty stations in the fleet. I was headed to Maryland to work in a SCIF on Fort Meade and Isaac was being sent to Hawaii. We decided to try a long-distance relationship. Or perhaps it was just me that insisted.

4

The Man Who Existed for Only a Day

At Fort Meade, I was assigned to a job completely devoted to the observation of secrets and reporting on those secrets while working inside one of the most secretive compounds in the world: the National Security Agency which we ominously called The Building. The first time I laid eyes on it was from the passenger seat of my roommate's car, just inside the pocket of a cloverleaf interchange on the Baltimore-Washington Parkway. All that I could see from the highway was a plain series of interconnected office buildings but as we drove through the gates, The Building greeted us with the full impact of its two massive, black box structures standing like dark sentinels on the other side. Their mirror-like, one-way black glass walls reflected the sea of vehicles packed across the yawning parking lots before them. As we checked in and drove towards the Marine detachment, my roommate casually mentioned that the structures were completely coated in copper shielding to prevent espionage. A forbidding feeling settled into my gut.

As you can probably guess, my job was of a sensitive nature and I am unable to write much about its details so the following information includes only what can be easily googled as well as my personal thoughts and feelings while in that role. Like my childhood, the need for secrecy has echoed the ever-present narrative of needing to control information, though, in this case, national security is a much better reason than "because I said so." Still, when I look back at all the ways the universe has tried to get my attention over the years it's pretty wild how blatantly obvious the language of repetitive symbolism has permeated my life.

The Marines of my company were assigned to various joint-task-force environments in The Building with civilian workers, contractors, and military personnel from other branches of service. As a signals intelligence (SIGINT) Marine, I worked in a system that collected, processed, analyzed, produced, and disseminated SIGINT information that directly supported the safety and security of the US and its allies. Once I was given a specific function, I found myself working as the only Marine on my team and one of only a handful on our entire floor which meant that my section leader was not a part of my Marine Corps chain of command.

Most of my enlistment entailed keeping one foot rooted in the Corps with the other in The Building. On a typical day, I'd meet up with some Marine friends at the chow hall for breakfast before walking across the vast ocean of parking lots to The Building, switching into work mode as I reported to my non-Marine section lead who would then relay back to my Marine command that I had made it into my seat. I was constantly being loaned out through a weird game of bureaucratic telephone. I'd work a full day with my team in The Building, head out to PT with my Marine friends after work and then enjoy the evening as I saw fit, barely interacting with my Marine Corps superiors at all. In the beginning, I only ever saw my command when we had full-company PT sessions about once a week and at Friday afternoon formations before being released for the weekend. It was incredibly bizarre as far as military enlistment experiences go.

While the lack of oversight continued to catapult me into a space of self-exploration and personality redefinition (which I greatly needed in order to process those childhood experiences), it also contributed to a growing feeling of isolation. A heavy weight quickly began to settle itself around my shoulders like a cloak, putting pressure on all those childhood secrets that were eating away at the hole in my heart. My work in The Building was beginning to take a mental toll.

As an observer of information I saw things I never wanted to see, knew things I never wanted to know, and basically served as a living, breathing, human garbage filter. I observed some of the worst things humans could do to each other and then wrote reports on what I observed—someone had to do it—but I never got to experience resolution for what I saw. The "bad guys" seemingly never paid the consequences. Some people in my job were able to truly handle it but the part of me that may have been able to process those pieces of information was already bursting at the seams from all the trauma I'd boxed up and filed away in my childhood. I was running low on internal storage and everything was starting to glitch.

While my brain was overflowing with humanity's informational garbage, my personal relationships began to rot in the bin. I started letting more and more of my mom's phone calls go to voicemail, completely cut contact with my dad, essentially choosing a side in their divorce, and limited communication with my siblings because I still felt incredibly guilty. But like an old Billy Mays commercial, "That's not all!" and the shitstorm kept piling on when Isaac called to end our long-term relationship—he had slept with someone else. I was devastated and snapped into full-on cling mode, grasping for the life raft I thought our relationship could still be. I convinced him to get on a plane and visit a few months later. We got back together as I spewed out lies of forgiveness only to find out that his fling had given him chlamydia and, therefore, had now given me chlamydia as well. My sense of self-worth plummeted to an all-time low. Thankfully, the nurse at medical was incredibly sweet, took extra time to sit and talk with me for a bit before pouring out a cup of strong, banana-smelling liquid that I needed to drink, and packed me off with a week's worth of doxycycline. If only there were antibiotics to clear up memories as well.

With the informational shitload pulling down my work life, declining familial connections, bubbling traumatic memories, and the uncertainty of my first real romantic relationship, the difficult months narrowed into dreadful weeks which turned into agonizing days. Every moment became excruciatingly painful as the weight of all the horrible secrets began to stack up in a precariously assembled mental Jenga. My inner vision narrowed and soon I was only capable of seeing the world through a veil of persistent horror, pain, and suffering.

Each morning I'd pour every ounce of energy into fighting back my own horrible secrets just to get out of bed and walk into The Building that mined the wretched secrets of others. I started to

notice other people on my new-found frequency, civilian workers that clung to the edges of the crowded hallways and wore
their own cloaks of depression for whatever they, themselves, had
seen. There was Bag-Head-Guy, a paranoid man who disguised
his identity by wearing a brown paper bag on his head at all times
with eye holes he'd roughly cut out with scissors (literally, he's a
real person). There were the Wall Touchers, singular individuals
who always traveled through The Building with a finger feathering
along the wall beside them, a grounding rod for their reality and a
physical confirmation that this place was indeed real. And when
I walked to the windowed common areas I'd see the Window
Lickers solemnly staring out the clear glass, trying to spy some
inner peace that lay outside The Building's walls. Day by day, I
became one of them.

The day I broke started out like any other. I dragged myself out
of bed, forced half of a bagel sandwich down my throat and walked
into The Building to fill my seat.

Shortly after checking in, a Navy Petty Officer I didn't recognize
stopped by my desk and asked me to come with him. My stomach
sank, knowing something wasn't quite right, but he outranked me
so it wasn't a question. I followed him into a small, windowless
meeting room and saw our section leader sitting behind a table.
Instantly I knew this was a "you fucked up" conversation and my
heart began to beat with the rhythm of panic.

"Lance Corporal," my section leader began, "some concerns
have been brought to my attention regarding your performance..."

Fuck.

He paused, shifting to look uncomfortably at his friend the Petty Officer as I stared straight ahead, not trusting myself to move an inch lest I burst into tears. I was completely out of the energy I needed to pretend that I was ok. His friend decided to speak up.

"Lance Corporal... are you ok?" the Petty Officer asked with surprising gentleness.

That single question tipped the scales. I was done for. The girl who wanted to be a big, tough Marine, who would rather die than show weakness, especially in front of men, had snapped, breaking into a million mental shards of glass. In the blink of an eye, tears started pouring down my face and they didn't stop. The deepest wells of my emotional pain had seen and experienced enough of what humans could do to each other and the black liquid of infinite anguish bubbled up from my depths in heavy, soul-wracking sobs. It took everything I had to try and keep the noise down, embarrassment and humiliation being the only parts of me struggling through the mental alarms for some level of control.

I split at the seams. I was both there in that room and not there at the same time. I was both sitting in my seat crying and standing next to this girl wearing a Marine Corps uniform who looked like she'd been through hell. I didn't recognize her. Then, a thought popped into my head. It was the perfect day for a hike and all I needed was a nice bit of rope and a good sturdy tree that could hold me. I didn't know where the thought came from or for how long I'd been thinking it but somehow it felt familiar, like greeting an old friend.

Suddenly, a warm hand held mine and gently squeezed. Somewhere in the ether a man started audibly breathing in a hypnotically deep rhythm, steadily coaxing my own breath to follow.

Gradually, my breathing slowed to match his. Coming back into a sense of semi-awareness I saw the face of the Petty Officer I had just met sitting in the seat next to me with a look of pure, selfless compassion. He existed, in this moment, entirely for me.

The section leader went off to find some tissues and, with a kindness I never expected, his friend helped me gather the fragments of my mind into a patchwork that could keep me together long enough to make it out of The Building. After I wiped my face and waited for the redness to subside, our section leader signed me out for the day telling my team that some "family stuff" had come up which wasn't a total lie. I gathered my belongings and, once again, followed the Petty Officer I had just met out into the parking lot.

I can't explain it, but I knew I could trust him implicitly. I felt like I knew him from somewhere. He walked me out to a truck that still had dealer's license plates and that new-car smell filled my senses. We drove silently across the base and traveled down a road I didn't recognize. I rolled the window down and closed my eyes as the sunlight danced through the shadows of conifer trees, drawing patterns behind my eyelids in the breeze that rustled their pine needles—my favorite sound.

If there's a God, I thought, *the music of whispering pines must be his favorite.*

We pulled into a small parking lot in front of an old building that read "Fleet and Family Services."

"There's someone here who might be able to help you," the Petty Officer said.

That's nice, I thought, *but there's no need because I'll be dead soon.*

As if hearing my thoughts read aloud, he turned in his seat to hold my gaze. "I'm not leaving your side until we're ok," he said. "Understand? Whatever it is, it'll be ok. We'll get there."

Why is he saying 'we'? I thought. I gave him a sad smile and followed him through the doors. We didn't have an appointment so we needed to wait. He sat next to me for almost an hour before a woman approached with a perfectly calculated smile—not too big, not too small—and beckoned me back to her office "for a chat."

It'll all be over soon, I mentally repeated. *You can do this. It'll all be over soon.*

And then it *was* over, though, not in the way I had anticipated. She talked me out of my hiking trip and gave me the processing space I didn't know I needed. I can't recall exactly what we talked about nor do I remember her name but I do know that I felt a sense of relief.

When we finished an hour later the petty officer was there waiting for me. He handed me a sandwich that he'd scrounged from the commissary down the road while I was in my session. I couldn't taste the turkey and cheese but I didn't need to, its purpose was sustenance. I directed him to my barracks and as we pulled up he jotted down his number on a slip of paper and handed it to me (which I promptly lost). Not quite sure what to say, we both sat there in silence for a bit longer with the engine running until I mustered the strength to walk inside.

"Thank you," I said, turning to look at him. "I think..." But I couldn't finish the sentence.

Shaking my head and thanking him again I walked up to my room before crashing on the bed with my boots still on. I was alive and that's all that mattered.

I never saw him again and, sometimes, I wonder if he only existed for that day, an angel sent by the universe to keep me alive. Petty Officer, from the bottom of my heart, thank you.

I only lasted ten months in that job and never saw my team in The Building again. The section leader had informed my command that I was no longer fit for duty and I found myself back in "Casuals," the holding platoon that all newcomers in our Marine detachment are a part of as they wait for their polygraphs and security clearances to pass before being assigned to a seat in The Building. I had no job, no function, and no purpose. I could have easily given up and allowed the humiliation of failure to consume me, sinking into the lowest ranks of oblivion but I'm a naturally resilient person and, weirdly, an optimist in only the darkest of times, so I picked my head up and tried what I could to make myself useful. A part of me knows that my command was trying to give me a mental break (I wasn't the first Marine to return from The Building) but I couldn't stand just sitting around so I voluntarily started assisting the admins in our company headquarters.

I became the company clerk and took part of the responsibility for Casuals platoon. Really, there was nothing to do in Casuals except wait and every day they went through the same routine: gather in the Duty Hut after breakfast, go PT as a group, come back after lunch, and clean or sit around until dismissal. There are jokes aplenty in the military about low-ranking individuals having to do the stupidest tasks imaginable just to make it look like we're putting tax dollars to work and Casuals was where some of those jokes became reality. We went around quads picking up individual cigarette butts by hand, moved furniture from one end of a building to another and back again for no real purpose, and cleaned clothes drying machines with cue-tips just to look busy. One time we were even instructed to vacuum the parking lot (and we literally did). It was 50% bullshit, 50% hurry-up-and-wait, and 100% Marine Corps.

The main complaint from the Marines stuck in Casuals platoon was the lack of direction and sense of meaningful fulfillment so I started organizing volunteer opportunities for the Marines-in-waiting with the Master Gunnery Sergeant's approval, allowing them, if they wanted, to get out and do some good instead of re-cleaning the things they had just cleaned yesterday.

I started to carve out a place for myself that wasn't rooted in the daily exposure to human garbage and continued to explore and express what the idea of personal identity meant to me. I formed several close friendships with my fellow Marines, started a *Dungeons & Dragons* group as Dungeon Master Niemenator, got into heated *Star Wars* and *Harry Potter* discussions in the company office, and generally made it my business to bring out as much joy, nerdiness and personality from our Marines as I could. I knew I succeeded when Master Guns himself one day admitted to being a DM in his youth before smirking back at us and huffing "fuckin' nerds" on his way out the door.

Veterans and active duty military members alike usually scoff at "pencil pushers," diminishing their necessary function because it lacks propagandic glory, so I focused my day-by-day existence in salvaging what respect I could. As the next year went by, I steadily became the back-end organizer, ensuring that our company of Marines got where they needed to be at the time that they needed to be there. Hilariously, and to the delight of many of my friends, I became a fulcrum point in our company's Lance Corporal Underground, a term used to describe how the lowest ranking Marines somehow always know everything in their command before it's officially announced. Was there going to be a surprise 7-mile company run the next morning designed to throw off unwary lance corporals? Not on my watch—everyone would be informed well beforehand so they could get a good night's sleep and a carb-loaded dinner. Staff Sergeant Morrelis got a DUI last night? Not to fear, everyone's already prepared for the company-wide lock down coming this weekend. But the power of the Lance Corporal Underground is perhaps best understood by observing the day my roommate called me from The Building with a warning that Lance Corporal Marconi had forgotten his ribbons and couldn't leave to get them from his barracks room because he was already in the middle of a sensitive operation. A uniform fault like that, if noticed by the right people, could make the whole company suffer collective punishment, therefore, it was in everyone's best interest to help our fellow Marine (though we all gave him shit for it later). With a little encouragement, one of the lance corporals in Casuals agreed to loan his own, identical ribbons for the day, taking off his uniform to head out to a volunteer opportunity off base. I found a runner with the right security clearance to get the ribbons to Marconi and then we waited. Master Guns stared at me from the doorway with narrowed eyes two hours later.

"A friend of mine in The Building called this morning to let me know one of my Marines had a fucked-up uniform but when I got there to berate the ever-loving shit out of him there was nothing to correct. Know anything about that, Niemer?"

Mirth flickered in his eyes. *It worked.*

"No, Master Guns, I don't know anything about a Marine being out of uniform right now."

Technically that wasn't a lie, he *was* currently wearing the right uniform.

"Hm, sure" he grunted, barely covering his smirk before walking away.

Crisis averted.

I honestly enjoyed my time as the company clerk but no matter how much I enjoyed it, I still felt the sting of failure gnawing away at the back of my mind, knowing that I'd never be able to fulfill my original purpose. Elements of sleep paralysis began to creep into my nightmares with more regularity. The demon that had been watching me from the corner of the ceiling in Pensacola had slowly started making his way forward to stand at the foot of my bed and I'd wake from those nightmares with a powerful urge to shake things up and do something else with my enlistment before it was over.

I decided that I needed to deploy.

Even though I had been let go from my team in The Building, I think my command had still intended to find another place for me but just hadn't gotten around to it. A year later my security clearance was still intact, I still had the right badges, I got promoted to the rank of corporal, and, most importantly, I had recovered some sense of self-respect by voluntarily taking on work for the company and not giving up. My resilience had been noticed.

So, like most of my life in retrospect, the right opportunity seemingly appeared out of thin air at the right time. My friend Murphy was deploying as a logistics NCO (Non-Commissioned

Officer) for his team and they needed someone to fill his position after he returned. We put our heads together to figure out how to get me into that vacancy. I interviewed with a Navy Chief that headed the group, talked to my Marine command about how this deployment would be "using resources wisely," and before I knew it I was receiving certifications to drive forklifts and climb cell towers, weaving my way through a special weapons course, and finding myself on a plane overseas just after Christmas.

5

Afghanistan

What the fuck am I doing here? I thought, as turbulence rocked the plane and the contractor who had unbuckled himself ten minutes after takeoff comically hit the bare metal floor with a thunk. Back on the ground he had boasted that this was his fifth tour in Afghanistan and that these flights were our last minutes to chill before pulling sixteen-hour days but he certainly didn't look relaxed now. I suppressed a laugh, watching as he sheepishly clambered back into his seat and strapped in. Captain Pereira snorted with derision though I thought I saw a glint of humor in his eyes through the dim red cabin lights of our midnight flight.

A voice came over the ICS. "Buckle up. We're preparing to land."

I strained against the harness that strapped me into the wall of the C-130 and attempted to look out the window but there was only blackness at 0100 hours.

When we landed the airstrip was full of activity. It may have been the middle of the night but our operation was continuous. The captain and I quickly grabbed our bags and made for the exit. Two members of our team were waiting for us and quickly walked us off the tarmac to a big, red Dodge Ram 3500 and, yes, it was completely out of regs. As we climbed in and drove off to our compound I asked myself once again, *What the fuck am I doing here?*

Less than four hours after we landed our base took mortar fire. I was in the conex box container room I'd just been issued as a living space and hadn't yet figured out what the protocol was though I did know that our rooms were covered by a protective layer the rest of the base didn't have. I thought I remembered someone saying it was safer to stay put if I were already in here. Sirens wailed as the mortars impacted and the small speaker in my room blared to life.

"INCOMING! INCOMING! INCOMING! IDF IMPACT. SHELTER IN PLACE AND DON IBA."

I pulled on my IBA (Individual Body Armor a.k.a. flak and kevlar) and listened closely. No one was running to the concrete shelters and I heard a few people talking through the walls of the containers next to me so I figured it was indeed safe enough to stay here. Forty-five minutes later we received the all clear and the Navy Chief who'd interviewed me for this position knocked on my door. Thankfully, I'd done everything relatively correctly. We could stay in our rooms if we were already there but I needed to check in with my team lead as soon as the all-clear sounded. Chief left and I tried to shake it off like everyone else and fall back asleep. I was unsuccessful.

Everything about my time in Afghanistan was the exact opposite of what a typical Marine Corps deployment looked like. For starters, our team was, once again, a joint-taskforce just like my prior team in The Building. We consisted of two Marines (myself and the Captain), the Navy Chief, and several other branches of the military with civilians and contractors thrown in for good measure—a completely mixed bag of assets. Additionally, my pre-deployment training had been through The Building, not the Corps, I was issued a Glock and an M-4 carbine by The Building instead of the typical M16 rifle and Beretta combo (though low-ranking enlisted Marines are rarely issued handguns unless they're military police), and I was explicitly told that I didn't need to report to the Marine Corps detachment here, though the Captain insisted we check in with them anyways. So when I walked into the Marine detachment offices after the Captain for check-in, explaining first to the deskbound admin Corporal and then to his superiors that I was *not* going to report for muster with the command here because I had "other assignments," the Master Sergeant at the end of the office didn't quite know what to do with me.

"Why do you think you're so special, Marine?" he asked, eyes flicking first to my hair, then to my uniform, looking for something to be out of regs that he could use as a weapon of opportunity in our pending verbal spar.

"I don't think I'm special, Master Sergeant. I'm just here to do my job." Hopefully the ease of my parade rest conveyed the confidence I needed to de-escalate this. I glanced toward the door the Captain had disappeared through and hoped he'd be done soon.

"Why's your pistol out of regs, Marine?" his eyes narrowed dangerously. "That Glock wasn't issued to you by the Corps."

"No it wasn't, Master Sergeant."

"Well what're you doing here, Corporal?"

"I'm checking in, Master Sergeant."

Oh fuck, you know that's not what he's asking, dumbass, I thought.

"Obviously," he drawled.

An image of Professor Snape popped into my head and I swallowed the joke that threatened to burst out of my lips. Bearing was never my strong suit.

"I'm the logistics NCO for my team and taking over management of our warehouse, Master Sergeant."

"And what does your team do?"

This was a question I didn't know how to answer. I wasn't explicitly told *not* to say anything to this man but when you work for The Building less is always more and I didn't want to fuck this up.

"Uh..." I stumbled over the right words, "I... we, we work with communications equipment."

It wasn't a lie.

"Corporal Niemer!" called a voice from my left. I turned with relief to see Captain Pereira exiting the room across the hall.

"Morning, sir," the Master Sergeant acknowledged. "You here with this Marine?"

"Yeah, she's with me so we won't be in your hair too much." I pursed my lips together—the Master Sergeant had none.

"Well she'll need to check in daily like the rest of 'em."

"She won't have time for that; we have a lot to do," the Captain corrected.

"All *enlisted* Marines answer to me on this base, Captain."

A couple of Marines in the vicinity slowed their pace to eavesdrop on the pissing contest.

"Yes, all Marines assigned to this division, but we have different orders. You can take it up with the Major if you'd like," he said, gesturing to the room he just exited.

"I don't like it," the Master Sergeant said. It was neither a continuance of the conversation nor was it an argument. He stated it as a fact and immediately walked across the hall to speak with his superior officer, shutting the door behind him.

Captain Pereira: 1 | Master Sergeant: Snape

"C'mon," the Captain waved.

"Uh, sir, he didn't dismiss me."

"*I'm* dismissing you."

"Right! Yessir!" My legs sprang into action as I followed him back outside.

"What was that all about?" Chief asked as we climbed into the truck.

The Captain didn't answer, firing back another question instead.

"Did Murphy check in with them?" He asked, jerking his thumb back towards the Master Sergeant.

"Nah," the Chief shrugged, "I told him it was unnecessary. He's been flying under the radar and it's worked out for us so far."

Chief didn't give a fuck.

The Captain let it go. Sometimes you don't want to know all the answers. We flashed our badges as we pulled up to our compound and carried on.

Driving forklifts around a warehouse full of communications equipment had its perks because I was also the person who retrieved all our mail and on day number one I learned that Amazon would ship pretty much anything anywhere in the world with the right address. In twenty days or less you could hold whatever you wanted in your own hands even on deployment (if it passed the inspectors and wasn't fresh produce). This information was considered so important by every member of our team that it was practically a part of my official onboarding and the more time passed the more we ordered the most random-ass shit for delivery.

It was like Christmas every week. We ordered non-perishable food items like pop tarts, cereal, pizza sauce and bagged pepperonis for pizza night, plenty of books and movies, and ridiculous costumes for the base fun-runs (Chief once volun-told us to run a 10k with him and even though I hated running I wore a stormtrooper onesie for it). But no one ordered from Amazon better than Williams who, as a joke, somehow got a massive pink dildo past inspection and suctioned it to Chief's desk just before breakfast about two months in. Shouts filled the office and everyone roared with laughter at the look on his face! The dildo moved around for a while after that, turning up in unlikely places with various shouts of disgust and cackles of glee.

Williams was my partner in crime and a good friend of Murphy's who made sure to introduce us on our way to the chow hall my first morning there. He was easily likable, funny, and talkative but nothing prepared me for the ride back to our compound after that first meal.

"Murphy, I need you to step on it," Williams said, his face paling as he leaned forward and gripped the sides of his seat.

"Dude, seriously! Already?" Murphy sighed dramatically as he acquiesced and picked up speed.

"Oh shit oh shit oh shit...." Williams looked like he was about to explode.

"Are you ok?" I asked, genuinely concerned.

"PULL OVER, MAN! IT'S COMING *NOW*!"

Murphy burst into giggles and pulled off onto the wrong side of the road. There was a porta-potty ahead but he stopped well short of the runner's shitter... on purpose.

"FUCK YOU!" Williams screamed as he threw open the door and ran like a penguin as fast as he could.

Murphy descended into howls of laughter, both at the look on my face and at Williams' run, trying to explain what was happening through gasping breaths.

"He has... he has... he has a *botox butthole*!" Humor consumed him.

"He has a *what*?" I asked, truly at a loss on this one.

"A BO-TOX BUTT-HOLE!" he shouted, unable to contain himself. He draped his heaving body over the wheel, smacking the dash and having the time of his life. As I tried to process this new phrase, Williams began his solemn trek back to the truck, cheeks flushed red once again, though this time with a sheepish look on his face.

"You asshole," he laughed, punching Murphy hard in the arm as he got back in the truck. "That was close!"

"Tell her about your *botox butthole*!"

He turned to face me with a dramatic flourish. "A few years ago when I was trying to put something away on the top of a pallet rack I slipped and the crate fell with me, landing on my stomach and perforating my intestine. I thought I was fine until the pain became unbearable. I got really sick, and actual feces started leaking out of my belly button a couple days later. I realized I was probably dying and when I got to medical they had to transfer me to a civilian hospital where I underwent emergency surgery. When I woke up I had a newly constructed butthole and a lot less intestine. TA-DA!" he concluded with jazz hands.

"Every day it's a race back from the chow hall!" Murphy sang cheerily, clearly enjoying his role as chauffeur. They cackled in the front seats as I digested a term I'd never imagined hearing before: *botox butthole.*

Williams was the life of the party on our compound. He was the King of Comic Relief, bender of rules, and chutzpah behind our weekly pizza night. Every Sunday afternoon we'd buy naan at the bazaar for the crusts, run to the chow hall to load up to-go boxes with toppings from the salad bar (I was responsible for packing two full containers of shredded cheese), and then pull out the rotating pizza ovens from the warehouse goodies cabinet (courtesy of Amazon). The whole team would gather for pizzas, sodas we borrowed from the chow hall, and our movie pick of the week.

Williams got me through the insanity of everything. He made the craziest, most fucked up shit somehow mentally digestible. He made me laugh more than I can remember and was funnier than I can ever do him credit for, helping everyone make light of the heaviest things. Everyone on deployment has a Williams but ours was, hands down, the best.

Of course, he was battling his own nightmares too (who wasn't?) but it was neither the time nor place to get sucked into them. We had a job to do so we shoved our nightmares and sleep paralysis demons down, saving them for later, and focused on the laughs instead.

I jolted awake as the speaker on the ceiling in my room shouted again.

"INCOMING! INCOMING! INCOMING! IDF IMPACT! TAKE COVER!"

Oh fuck, here it comes. I thought, tensing up as I grit my teeth.

BOOM

BOOM

BOOM

Three mortars hit the base. The walls of my conex box rattled like they were back on a freight train. I rocked myself back and forth, trying to pretend like everything was ok and this was totally normal. The mortars had hit just before I was about to walk out the door and start my day. I could have died. Finally, we were given the all clear and I walked over to our main office of operations after calming my breath.

"Niemer!" Chief called as soon as I entered, "I'm assigning you to a quick mission with Mike tomorrow. He's gotta fix some equipment out in the field. You'll be the muscle packing heat."

"Sounds good, Chief!" I nodded.

Mike was a contractor and contractors weren't allowed to carry weapons anymore—there'd been too many weapons discharges, meaning too many contractors had shot at stuff (or people) without authorization. Military personnel were always assigned to travel with them now for safety and security purposes. I was his battle buddy. But Chief had a weird look on his face, like something wasn't quite right, so I hovered near his desk until he looked up at me again.

"I don't know how to say this, Niemer, but... well, I'm sorry. We didn't really have another option. Everyone else has something important they gotta do tomorrow. I can't go, the Cap'n can't go..."

"What is it, Chief?" I asked, sensing that something was pretty wrong.

"Well, you're a woman and..." Black rage exploded defensively through my heart. "... and women technically aren't supposed to be sent to this location. It's a different sort of place..." he trailed off uncomfortably.

"Just promise me you guys will hurry and make it back before dark. You *have* to leave before dark. Got it? Women aren't allowed to stay after dark."

Oh. He's not trying to be a sexist dick, this is some serious shit. I understood.

"Will do, Chief. We'll be quick."

"Good," he nodded. "You make sure you do that."

The next day we dropped off some members of our team at another location on the way. Mike was cheery and looking forward to seeing a friend of his who had been stationed there to monitor the equipment we were fixing. But no amount of excitement from my coworker could override the intensity of Chief's warning. His voice echoed in my head and my body tensed as we leapt off the chopper and into another world.

Immediately I understood what he meant. I was the *only* woman at this outpost and every man we passed knew it. They didn't try to hide their curiosity, blatantly stopping in their tracks and staring at us. Mike and I locked eyes and picked up the pace. The men here followed my every movement and some even started following us on foot. The air thickened.

Perhaps it was my imagination but it felt like I had gained instant access to some hidden telepathic ability. Thoughts that *couldn't* belong to me started pouring through the cracks in my skull. Horrible thoughts.

We're gonna kill you.

I bet she'd put up a fun fight.

The audacity of this fucking American FEMALE.

We're gonna kill you.

You shouldn't have come here.

I'd love to get my hands around that throat...

We're gonna kill you.

I wanted to vomit. The weight of the Glock on my hip and the M-4 in my hands grew heavier with a sense of imagined reassurance. We weren't at war with these men but they were at war with me.

Keep your finger straight and off the trigger, Meg. Straight and off the trigger. Deep breaths.

Mike gave me a sideways look of acknowledgment and moved closer to me. Either he could hear them in his head too or everything was so incredibly obvious that we were about to be in some deep shit.

"Mike!" A voice shouted from behind a group of men who were getting closer. Mike's friend, blessedly, had found us.

Taking in the situation he pushed through the crowd and hung his arms around both of our shoulders in a very friendly, very American display of ease, whisking us away from the imminent detonation and into the building that held our equipment. We got to work. I helped where I could but Mike was the technician here, not me, so I passed the solder and wires and dealt with the echoes of assaulting thoughts. After six hours of passing tools over to Mike, taking water breaks, and deep breathing to pass the time, I was at a mental breaking point. My body was running on empty after pushing adrenaline for half a day straight. We finished early, a whole hour before the chopper could come back for us, so we holed up in a small room out of sight to wait in silence. I made sure to stay away from the windows, only really breathing again when we were strapped into the helicopter and on our way back.

"Niemer, you good?" Mike shouted over the beating rotors. "That felt fuckin' crazy!"

"Yeah, I'm good!" I lied, breaking out a shaky smile as I tried to convince him. "That *was* crazy! You fixed that bitch in record time though. Chief'll be happy!"

Mike beamed and smiled back at me. The telepathic voices faded into the distance but, somehow, the intensity of their energy had rooted in the shadowy recesses of my mind, giving them a new foothold in my nightmares. I didn't sleep that night and struggled to sleep in the weeks after. My old sleep paralysis demon became many demons, minions of dread, and all of them wanted to kill me.

(*Exploration and Interpretation, Sleep Paralysis*)

A month later Mike and I were headed out on a mission again, but this time the location was safer (meaning only that there were other women stationed there) so we'd be spending a few nights. We loaded our gear into a fixed-wing, bare-bones Cessna and headed up over the mountains. The metal protested with every shift in position and I was pretty sure we were going to shake ourselves out of the air during takeoff but once we evened out my heart rate lowered.

Somewhere on that flight, I slipped out of time and space. Perhaps it was the beauty of the snowcapped mountains or the deep blue of the sky that resembled my favorite stone, lapis lazuli. Either way, the scene outside my window was magickal. The shadow of the Cessna danced upon the icy ridges, adjusting its size and shape to slip along the slopes of ancient crevasses. A golden eagle circled off in the distance. The beauty of Earth took my breath away.

We got right to work after landing, ate some dinner, went to bed, took some mortar fire, woke up, and worked again, following suit just like the day before. I forget exactly how many days we were there because it didn't really matter. All that mattered was finishing the job and taking shelter when the mortars dropped.

The morning Mike and I were scheduled to return quickly spun into a whirlwind of events as two high-ranking pilots walked into the makeshift airport and made a beeline for us.

"You Mike and Megan?"

Who the fuck gave these guys my first name? And why the fuck are they using it?

"Yeah, that's us." Mike's eyes narrowed.

"It's your lucky day, we're flying you back on the Learjet. Someone's plans changed at the last minute but it's already fueled and ready to go. We gotta burn it."

Mike's mouth hit the deck as I stared straight ahead not wanting to show how gullible I was to believe this might actually be happening.

"Well," the pilot said, interrupting our silence and pointedly checking his watch. "Are you coming? We don't have all day."

Mike elbowed me in the ribs. We followed them out onto the tarmac and saw the bougiest jet I would never have imagined myself flying in. My brain blared warning sirens. *Is this a joke or is this really ok? Am I going to get in trouble for boarding this thing?*

But Mike was a contractor without the threat of Captains and Chiefs and was so excited by our turn of fortune that he hopped gaily up the stairs to plop himself into a tan leather seat without any need for further encouragement.

"Look!" he giggled, opening a bag on the table next to him, "Donuts!"

He wasn't wrong, we each had a bag of fresh donut holes and a cup of hot coffee on the trays next to our seats.

What the actual fuck is happening? I wondered.

Soon the pilots started flipping switches and driving us onto the runway, checking with the tower that we were cleared for takeoff. The revving engines made a thrumming sound inside the craft.

"You two ever experience a combat take-off?" one of the pilots shouted back at us.

"No!" We yelled out at the same time.

"Well buckle up and enjoy it!"

We began to accelerate quickly. Way too quickly. We were about to smash into the blast wall but the G-forces kicked in and the whole world flipped ninety degrees backwards in an instant. We blasted straight up into the air, one second parallel to the ground, the next perpendicular. I tried to lift up my arms just to see if I could but they were as heavy as lead. My cheeks felt like they were pulling down and I laughed at what I imagined my face to look like as we shot upwards on the world's fastest and most expensive roller coaster.

When we reached altitude and evened out I readjusted in my seat to look out the window and immediately felt moved to tears.

I could see space.

It wasn't *space* space but I could see the undeniable curvature of the Earth's surface, the delineated layers of the atmosphere, light blue far below darkening into navy and then the black of nothingness above.

I could see stars in the middle of the day.

Again, like our flight in, I felt myself slipping into a space beyond time as I stared out the window. I heard the pilots asking me if I had any questions or if I wanted to unbuckle and see the cockpit but their words didn't register until after we landed. I was somewhere else. I was off in space. (Years later, I would begin to recall bits and pieces about where I went. I had left not only my body, but the planet, finding myself in a different sort of craft outside of the human experience.)

And then we were touching down again, slammed back into reality in an instant. It felt like only a minute had passed but we were hundreds of miles away and headed back to work.

That night was, for the first time since I'd stepped foot in Afghanistan, totally free of nightmares.

I spent my twenty-third birthday shirking my duties by writing a D&D homebrew campaign in the cool, air-conditioned warehouse I managed, and complaining to anyone who popped in that I was supposed to be back in the States already. My childish sulking felt justified. Birthdays were meant to be celebrated but it's hard to celebrate when mortar fire takes a chunk out of the runway hours before you're supposed to get on a flight home and two days before your birthday. It's not that my birthday wasn't celebrated, Chief and the team cut slices of a makeshift cake and sang to me that Sunday pizza night like we had for so many others, but I wasn't able to celebrate it *my* way: getting drunk with my friends back in Maryland. Instead, I spent the next week in a checked-out mental fog acting as childishly annoying as possible without risking a write-up, hoping they'd pull some strings to get me on the next available flight home just to rid themselves of me. They didn't (literally they couldn't), and by the time I finally felt the slight stickiness of tar on a hot runway under my boots the sour taste of self-loathing and regret lingered on my tongue.

But I wasn't back in the US yet, I was unloaded and filtered into the barely-moving check-in line of a military base in Qatar, my halfway point. After getting my papers squared away I walked quickly across the base to my assigned squad bay to wait for a flight back to Maryland. I ducked into the cool, blacked-out interior of the building and felt around for the first available rack, not bothering to pull out a light or make any sense of organization for my equipment. I set an alarm and slipped below the surface into a dead sleep at the bottom of an exhausted, emotional sea. It was over.

I woke in a panic, grasping at the hands that pressed around my neck before realizing there was no one there. Air heaved itself in and out of my chest as I desperately recalled how to inhale and exhale, reaching for the metal bars of my rack, the cell phone under my pillow, or any other tangible object that could anchor me back into reality. I tried to shake the remnants of the nightmare off but the pressure of a growing migraine sloshed around in my head and my eyes recoiled from the harsh light of the cell phone that told me I had just a few hours before my ride came to take me to the airport.

Fuck. Just what I need... a migraine on a long-ass flight, I thought.

I knew I wasn't going to make it if I didn't try to salvage the situation. They had electrolytes at the chow hall. Stepping outside, the dry desert heat slammed into my body and I grimaced as the sunlight shot daggers through the portals in my skull. The intensity of the trek there drained any energy I had left but once I arrived, the cool interior was a wonderful blessing despite the sounds of clanging trays and shouting laughter clamping down on my migraine's halo in a vice grip of pain. I grabbed two Gatorades and two bananas before remembering that I had some foam earplugs in my pocket. Jamming them in, I traded the harshness of petty conversations for the intimacy of the sound that blood makes as it throbs against the sides of your brain. It wasn't necessarily better, just different, but that's all I needed. I pounded the Gatorades between chunks of banana on the way back and hoped the electrolytes and potassium would kick in fast.

Such luck was not mine that day.

The migraine persisted and worsened, making it hard to concentrate as one of my team's connections shoved my bags cheerily into the trunk of their car and talked my ear off as we exited the base. They were driving me to the civilian airport, Doha, and the journey sits somewhere in my memory like that Dalí painting of the melting clocks—weird and dream-like. Instead of timepieces strewn across a desert landscape, I took in a sea of massive chandeliers displayed within the windows of a desert metropolis. We passed shop after shop full of chandeliers. Some shops were even three stories high with floor-to-ceiling glass walls highlighting the sparkling, bejeweled light fixtures that stretched from the top floors to their entryways. I had never seen such massive and ornate pieces of light. It was beyond strange.

I interrupted the driver with a confused comment regarding the sheer amount of chandelier shops on this *one* road in this *one* city and was met with a roaring laugh that made me wince with pain as the sound echoed around the chamber of my pulsing head. They explained that chandeliers were a sort of a status symbol here, like an expensive car, and that people loved to host and show off their sometimes two-story tall works of lighting art. Though my driver had said many wild things on this drive, I chose to believe them because nothing else made sense.

After passing Chandelier Thoroughfare we pulled up to the airport and before I could comprehend where I was, my bags were on the ground and the driver was pealing away. I walked inside and my stomach immediately sank. For my extra week overseas, Chief had attempted to make it up to me by altering my original flight to a cushy, civilian one. Though this was nothing new for our team (he did it whenever possible for anyone departing), I immediately felt the exhaustive weight of my naivete—this was no place for me.

It was the fanciest, richest, cleanest airport I had ever stepped foot in and I understood why Chandelier Boulevard existed: this was a country of flagrant wealth. Everyone in the airport was toting expensive luggage and wearing gold jewelry, everyone except for me who was dragging two overly-packed camouflage bags and wearing my boyfriend's oversized blue flannel jacket. I was obviously American. So began the living nightmare. The two pieces of luggage I needed to check both exceeded the weight limit so the underdressed, American woman opened her deployment bags on the floor of the main entrance, under a massive crystal chandelier, to pull out a third, unused bag and redistribute all the contents for everyone to see. I felt incredibly stupid. Shame flushed my cheeks as I listened to whispers in a language I didn't understand and fought to stem back the tears that were clearly a result of my migraine and not just because I felt so exposed and alone. I just wanted to go home.

My now *three* bags passed the weight restrictions and were taken off my hands, the release of their burden was felt both physically and emotionally, though the whole ordeal had magnified my migraine into auric territory. Everything was starting to blur. I made my way into a convenience mart and found the medication section. They didn't have Excedrin but I did find Advil and purchased two packets. Sinking into a chair next to my terminal I swallowed the double dose, pounded another bottle of water, and closed my eyes, praying for mental solace. I was nudged awake by a woman sitting next to me and saw the boarding line forming. Shuffling through the throngs of people shoving their bags into overhead compart-ments I collapsed into my seat. The Advil had done nothing and the pain was beginning to wear down on every faculty I had. It Just. Wouldn't. End.

Two hours into the flight, the un-showered smell of some-one next to me became unbearable, sending me over the edge. I couldn't take the pain anymore. Tears tumbled freely down my cheeks. I stumbled back to the flight attendant area and asked if anyone spoke English. They didn't, so I began miming the pain that I was in and asking for anything, *anything* that would make it go away. They didn't have anything to sell but one woman took pity on me and held out an assortment of colorful pills in what I assumed was her own personal plastic baggie of goodies, handing me two capsules. I don't remember their color nor did I know what they were but I didn't care. I took whatever it was that she gave me and passed out shortly after.

By the time I woke up we were landing and my migraine was blessedly gone. I tried to thank her as she passed but she refused to look at me and I understood that I had just taken some sort of trip into the void and she needed me to forget about it. As my feet walked off the plane I looked around at the bland, dirty, simplistic space of an American airport and breathed a sigh of relief. Hopefully my command wouldn't select me for a post-travel urine test.

It was finally, *finally* over.

6
LOSS

Reintegrating after deployment wasn't as easy as I thought it would be. As soon as a friend picked me up from the airport in Baltimore I learned that our whole company of Marines had moved to a new barracks at the far end of the base and some of the belongings I had left with friends for safekeeping had been lost in the transition. I tried to shake it off, they were only possessions, but the feeling of loss settled in anyway. There was no way to return to the way things were. Everything was different. In the new building, I was assigned a new roommate and quickly learned that we were never meant to share a living space together. Everything about her was irritating—her music, her habits, the way she cleaned, the old, molding food she kept in our fridge, the way her ramen sprawled out onto my side of the cabinets—literally everything. Her resonance just didn't jive but, perhaps, it was also *me* that no longer jived with myself.

I tried finding some sense of normalcy but there was nothing normal to go back to. No longer concerned with just surviving in the moment, the weight of my deployment experiences piled on top of those from my childhood and from my time in The Building. All of this gravity was starting to make my heart collapse in on itself, forming a sort of black hole, and cracking me open. I could no longer ignore the dark truths that were begging for my attention from the shadows within my being. The sense of fulfillment and purpose that I had sought through deployment never came, instead, I descended further and further into the eternal void of emptiness, and down there, in the deepest of depths, I heard a grating truth: I had wanted my deployment to kill me.

I hadn't volunteered to help our mission succeed, I had selfishly wished that one of the planes or helicopters would be shot down so I wouldn't have to go for that hike in the woods after all. The impetus of that truth, that there was still something so horrifying in my life story that I couldn't bear to live, began to take a new physical form in my more dream-like recurring nightmares: the terrifying sea monster circling below me in the depths—*the leviathan*. The more often I saw its undulating body protruding from the waves, the more I understood that my deployment had all been a ruse to escape my body and everything it had suffered. I hadn't, in truth, wanted to come back at all. I had hoped, underneath the layers and layers of denial, that "the enemy" would take my life for me because I hadn't been able to do it myself. I tried not to think about digging into the camping box. I tried not to think about my last day in The Building. I tried not to think about whatever was stuffed in those mental boxes I had filed away all those years ago but the memories began to surface anyway. Maybe it *was* time.

I tried to shove it all down. I tried to just get over it. I tried *so hard* to be ok but nothing seemed to work. I knew I needed to talk to someone but I also felt completely incapable of doing so. I had a massive block of resistance to therapy. Part of it was the underlying narrative of the military and part of it was the innate sense of knowing that I wasn't yet ready to meet my leviathan—I would rather die instead.

I started coping with alcohol. I shoveled ounce after ounce of burning liquid into the hole in my chest, hoping to somehow drown the monstrous glowing eyes that stared at me whenever I slept even though the thing thrived in liquid in the first place. I wasn't completely alone in the darkness though, in fact, every friend that returned from overseas brought their own version of suffering to the party. Some of them were severely depressed, most had some form of PTSD, and many had begun to question who they really were and what they were doing with their lives which led to difficult answers. We had never seen combat and, therefore, didn't feel like we had earned the right to experience PTSD (so the narrative goes). Instead, we welcomed our friend Maker's Mark to the crew and amplified our individual senses of hollowness into a collective experience.

One morning I woke up after a late-night binge with friends lying on my stomach with the *Lord of the Rings* extended edition playing on a laptop next to my head. I smiled, watching as Frodo and Bilbo bounced around in the back of a wagon on their way to the Grey Havens.

Awareness set in slowly. I wiggled my fingers and toes, regained some feeling in my limbs, and felt something heavy pressing down on my back. As my head pounded with yet another migraine I groaned and tried to glance back at my surroundings. I was in my own bed and in my own room but my entire military closet had been emptied and lovingly rearranged atop my sleeping body in order of dress ascendency. Closest to my back lay my PT shirts and shorts followed by three pairs of desert cammies, three pairs of woodlands, my service charlies with pants, the service bravo shirt and skirt, service sweater, alpha jacket, and green women's neck tab, followed by my dress blue deltas with pants, dress blue charlies shirt and skirt, dress blue alpha jacket with medals (my ribbon stack was currently on my service charlies), blue neck tab, stiff, white alpha gloves, and, finally, gloriously, the wrinkled Inspector Gadget trench coat that someone had found stuffed in the bottom of a sea bag. The piss cutter had fallen off my head when I first moved to survey the weight, but my service and dress blue bucket covers lay on either side of my pillow, completing the pile of clothing that covered one of America's most honorable: a United States Marine. Oorah. Yut Yut. Semper fuckin' Fidelis.

Dragging myself out from under the stacked uniforms and onto the floor I didn't bother standing up, opting instead for a slow baby crawl to the fridge where I sat back and downed some orange juice straight from the plastic jug. Sam, Merry, and Pippen sniffled in the background as I surveyed the mess before me. My friends had waged war upon my room, rummaging through every crevice in their drunken stupor to complete the uniform mission Captain Morgan had assigned them.

Belligerent assholes, I thought.

After a few minutes of rest I slowly threaded the cap back onto the jug and hauled myself up to a standing position. The pounding in my head took a hot minute to subside but as my vision cleared, I gingerly made my way to the door and looked out into the hallway.

"Good morning, Gonzalez," I whispered, toeing the man that lay propped up against the wall to my left. He clutched a blue lightsaber in one hand and an empty shot glass in the other. Master Guns was right, we really were a bunch of fuckin' nerds.

"Semper fi, mothafucka," he said, opening his eyes for a brief second to salute me with sarcasm, clearly still drunk.

"What happened?"

"You threw up and passed out early," he mumbled. "The big green weenie stopped by to grace you with uniform magick. Do you feel held by our heavenly devil dogs? Have fun cleaning your room, sucka..."

I walked back inside and ran him some water from the bathroom sink. He looked back up at the sound of my returning footsteps and eagerly reached for the glass.

"You wanna hit the chow hall?" I asked. "Get some food in you?"

"Nah, imma just lay here a bit."

"If duty walks by and sees you sleeping outside my door we'll both get in trouble."

He sighed dramatically.

"Fine."

He set the water glass at my feet and crawled down the hallway on all fours, dragging the lightsaber with him and shoving the shot glass into a pocket. I decided I wasn't hungry. After throwing all my uniforms on the ground I went back to bed and sunk into nothingness.

A few weeks later every corporal in our battalion was enrolled in Corporals Course, a month-long mandatory leadership program. Initially I felt some excitement at the change of pace, an opportunity to get out of my head and into "real Marine Corps shit." We'd be spending a whole month with our fellow Marines for once, which would culminate in a field exercise but my friends were not so enthused and droned on in discontent. Any elation I had felt was quickly dashed as I seamlessly donned the echoes of their ire, choosing the collective mentality of resentment over self-development. The hole in my heart descended through the last layers of crusty material and plummeted into the caverns of my ancestral underworld. *This is just the way it is,* I told myself.

I no longer drank to fill the hole and drown the leviathan. I drank because that's just what we did.

In the last week of the course I showed up to our Friday morning formation hung over and wearing sunglasses while standing in the back with my arms crossed.

"Niemer, your sunglasses are out of regs," the Staff Sergeant warned.

"Technically, you haven't called formation yet, Staff Sergeant."

The frown on his face echoed my own sentiment of self-disappointment but I'd lost the rope to haul myself out at this point. The chuckles from my friends filled me with shame.

"Atten-tion!" he called.

I snapped the sunglasses off my face and clenched my hands at my sides, flinging the glasses onto the pavement at my feet in the process. His eyes narrowed, I was just quick enough to avoid a reprimand but we all knew it wasn't funny.

Don't worry, I thought in his direction, *I'm disappointed in me too.*

A month later it was time for the Marine Corps Ball. The annual ball celebrates the birthday of the Marine Corps (Nov. 10th,

1775) with a ceremony of military pomp and circumstance. It's both a traditional, somber event, honoring those who have come before us and a lively, celebratory one full of drink and dancing. At this point, I knew I wasn't re-enlisting and that this would be my last ball so I invited three special guests to attend with me: my (still) long-distance boyfriend, Isaac, my mom, and my mom's boyfriend. A part of me was subconsciously trying to revive some long-dead relationships, hoping I could salvage some form of love in my life because I had none left to give to myself. It was the first time anyone in my family had wanted to visit me in Maryland.

Isaac needed some encouragement to attend. A Marine himself, he had recently EAS'd (reached his End of Active Service) and adamantly claimed that he was "just a civilian now." He wanted nothing to do with the Corps anymore but I managed to persuade him to go in the end. That night we both laughed at the irony as he, like always, buttoned up his dress blues jacket to the tune of ZZ Top's *Sharp Dressed Man*. Squaring our uniforms away, we met my mom and her boyfriend in the entrance of our hotel and walked over to the venue together.

I quickly got the sense that my mom loved the whole pomp and circumstance thing. Her boyfriend at the time was an Army veteran and he'd gotten his own dress uniform refitted specially for the occasion. She loved standing next to him, she loved standing next to me, pointing out the small menagerie of shiny medals on my chest, and she loved telling people that she was the one who raised me. A part of her boyfriend loved it as well. He lit up in his ASUs and regaled tales to young lance corporals about his time in Panama before they were even born but when I looked over at Isaac I saw a man who was still too close to it all to reminisce about his own deployment like "the good ol' days." We had that in common and I realized that I hadn't just badgered him into attending with me, I'd convinced him to put on the mask of a Marine once again and suffer in a misery that mirrored my own. Because while I was taking shelter from daily mortar fire and being sent with Mike to fix equipment in Afghanistan, he lay deep in the bowels of a Navy vessel and occasionally trudged through the jungles of east Asia on "training exercises."

The worst of his enlistment had come from his voluntary subjection to SERE's course, a product of the Vietnam war that prepared an individual to survive the worst of being a POW. He mentioned very little about his time in the course but, when he tried to paint a picture, only alluded to the basics which included being "placed in a small box for a few days" and "trying not to freeze after being stripped naked and submerged in an icy river." Isaac not only came back with pink and white scars lacing his spine like a haphazard shoelace but the mental scars to go with them. The drunken laughter and merriment of the festivities around us began to sound hollow.

We stocked up on drinks before settling at our tables and the ceremony began. Swords were raised, food for the dead was served, the Commandant's message was played, cake was cut, and the bell rang out again and again. The ball rolled on into merriment, laughter, and dancing. Isaac got a little too drunk a little too early and required assistance returning to our hotel room. I told my friends I'd be back soon after tucking him into bed but as we staggered our way out the door I could tell that something was off and possibly very wrong. It wasn't just the dark possessiveness in his eyes nor was it the typical anger in his voice, there was something simmering under the surface that I had never seen before. It remained elusive, swimming in and out of focus through his gestures and words, until we entered our room.

WHOOSH

The breath left my chest as my back slammed into the wall in the entryway. Confusion spread through my limbs, dulling my senses as I tried to comprehend what was happening.

THUD

I slowly turned my head to the right and saw that a fist had just punched the wall an inch from my face.

Huh. That's new, I thought.

Unhurriedly, I noticed that the fist was attached to an arm and that this arm was attached to a body and the body belonged to Isaac. I lifted my eyes to meet his gaze and sunk into the depths of two churning maelstroms screaming from an abyss of despair. I looked down, down, down into their turbulent waters until I spied the truth of the hole in his own heart. It was a pit, much like mine, with an empty cavernous system leading all the way back into his own ancestral underworld.

I saw him and I knew him.

I battled against the latent fear that threatened to blow up into panic, keeping our gaze locked, before gently wrapping my hands around the fist on the wall next to my head. I urged it slowly to lower and after a few seconds of resistance, guided it down to rest at its owner's side.

He blinked, saying nothing and turned to walk over to the bed before lying down to stare at the ceiling. I approached carefully, reading him just like I'd taught myself to do in childhood, and sensed the right action. I methodically began removing his uniform, unlacing his shoes, pulling them off, and placing them on the floor. My fingers unbuckled the white belt and unworked the golden buttons of his blues. I coaxed him to one side and slid out an arm then gently rolled him onto the other, removing the jacket this way and then the shirt. The khaki web belt came next followed by his trousers with their scarlet stripes—the blood of our fallen brothers at Chapultepec—until he lay there, defeated, in a white undershirt and boxer briefs. I picked up his feet and swiveled him right-way onto the bed before propping up the pillows and climbing in, placing my back against the wall and his head in my lap.

Tears streamed down his face as sobs began to wrack his body. No words were needed. I ran my fingers through his curls and held him when he was ready to sit up. We stayed like that for hours, and for hours I felt my thoughts floating in and out of that hotel room. Sometimes they were with us and sometimes they were far away in parallel universes where I had never met him. They went out like scavengers and came back with the same message that I had known for a while: it was time to go our separate ways.

The question was, could I do it?

I couldn't.

After that night I kept trying to find the right words to say, but whenever I was about to harness the courage to bring it up, the buried child within me cried out, terrified at the prospect of loss and only stalling the inevitable. She clung to the idea of him like I clung to the life raft in my sea of nightmares avoiding the knowing gaze of the leviathan that lurked below.

Our relationship was one of mutual suffering in which we each wanted to help the other but neither of us wanted to help ourselves. We maintained the cyclical family systems of thought we each carried, continuing to feed into the ancestral wounds that bound us to each other, the unspoken, unacknowledged wounds we each held onto. After the ball he went back to live with his parents in another state, only visiting occasionally when my asking turned into childish begging, drawing out our long-distance relationship well past its expiration date. The signs were all there, the red flags that called my attention regarding both his actions and my own began to compound, yet I just couldn't let him go. I couldn't let myself go. A part of me wished he'd take responsibility for both of us and just end it himself, handing me an opportunity to play the victim and coddle the panicking little girl in my head, distracting her from looking at the *real* wounds but we remained as we had been since the first time I saw his rage on display all those years ago in Texas—stuck.

Life carried on and somehow I got promoted to the rank of sergeant a month before my EAS date without really trying. It felt like a pity promotion more than anything. My inner conflict had continued to urge me to let go of our relationship but the little girl in my head won, so Isaac and I found ourselves packing up a small U-Haul trailer and waving to my roommates in Maryland as I became a civilian once again. There were no excuses left. It was now or never.

Cowardice won again on both sides as we pulled out onto the road. We threw some music on and drove 2,700 miles across the country from Baltimore to Seattle for a job I had landed working for the U.S. Army Corps of Engineers as a Natural Resources Specialist.

Seattle was beautiful in a way I'd never experienced before and you could find a view of "The Big One" from anywhere in the surrounding area. Mount Rainier dominated the landscape with its snow-capped dome and massive lenticular cloud, an eerie, upside-down saucer that looked like something out of a sci-fi movie. The mountain gazed down upon us, surveying its realm like a giant sentinel from some ancient world. It felt comforting.

We camped out in the bed of Isaac's truck for a week before finding a little studio apartment we could afford together just south of the city. It wasn't much bigger than a barracks room but it had everything we needed and, most importantly, it was ours. I was ready to start a new life with the man who had traveled with me and looked forward to building my own version of the American Dream. Each day I'd pull on the gray and green uniform of the Ballard Locks, lace up my black leather steel-toed boots, and thread the braided brown belt through the loops at my waist before shaking Isaac awake as I headed out for my afternoon-into-evening shift.

Traffic was shitty but never worse than it had been in Maryland and once I crossed Lake Union it usually calmed, releasing the tenseness I'd been gathering since the drive home the previous day. After badging into the gate and parking my truck I'd start my day with a walk through the botanical gardens, saying hello to the ancient sycamore before completing my rounds. According to my Fitbit, I usually walked an average of sixteen thousand steps in a shift. The Ballard Locks are one of the only lock and dam systems in the world that stand between freshwater and saltwater. I monitored the perimeter cameras, chatted with visitors across the lock's walkways, and checked on the salmon ladder, pointing out its total of twenty-one weirs to a never-ending sea of excited children on school trips. I truly loved every minute of it but at the end of each day a heavy dullness would throb against the walls of the pit that still lingered in my heart space as I entered our apartment and stepped into the two personal relationships that waited there: one with Isaac and another with the now ever-present leviathan.

In retrospect, I can see how the dullness grew with time. At first, numbness covered my fear as I asked Isaac if he'd had any luck on the job hunt each day. He hadn't and didn't want to talk about it but our funds were dwindling quickly and I knew we'd soon need a second income so I poked the bear as much as I dared, spending the rest of the evening in silence after our arguments. After a while, he did find a job but the dullness remained, replaced by a feeling of loneliness as he started working night shifts. He was gone before I came home and, after exchanging only a few brief words in the morning, would fall asleep as I tiptoed around the studio getting ready for work. Our relationship was once again characterized by the feeling of distance.

It was not the way I had wanted this to go.

The feelings of loneliness amplified and Isaac suggested we get a dog. I'd always wanted a dog and while I knew our studio apartment and limited funds created a less-than-ideal scenario for bringing a furry companion into the picture, I couldn't help the feelings of bubbling love and excitement at the suggestion. A few weeks later we came home from the pound with Mr. Roody-Roo, a boxer mix who had been born deaf and had a thick black line above his right eye like a massive, constantly questioning eyebrow. He was the derpiest looking dog and I loved him more than I had ever loved anything in my life. I got to work straightaway on his training, enjoying the time I spent looking up hand signals and learning how to communicate with him. He was a great dog but the feelings of loneliness resurfaced. I loved him, but Roody couldn't fill the hole in my chest.

I verbally acknowledged the loneliness, asking Isaac if there was any way he could work a few day shifts so we could actually see each other. He insisted that working nights was how everyone got started in his field and that he'd receive the opportunity for a normal schedule in time, plus, the night differential would help us financially. Unfortunately, it didn't help enough, and, as Trump was sworn into office, a federal hiring freeze dashed any hopes we'd had of financial security—the higher pay rate I had been promised after my probationary period completed never came to pass.

Our arguments became fights as we tightened our spending, trying not to panic. In an attempt to kill two birds with one stone I figured I could find a better-paying job that also had better hours with the State Park system and soon enough I turned in my two weeks' notice to the Locks and accepted a job at Dash Point with slightly better pay and a shift that started early in the morning. Finally, we'd have the evenings to spend together after my day ended and before Isaac's began with the bonus of a comfortable paycheck.

The change didn't manifest in the way I'd imagined and the more time we spent together the more I understood what I'd already known: we needed to go our separate ways.

As much as I knew this, I refused, again, to accept it. I clung desperately to a false reality, trying to force the vision of my life into a box that could neither hold its shape nor support its weight. My nightmares exploded, waking me every morning with the truth of our situation and the unprocessed feelings of fear that I could no longer afford to ignore. Every shitty thing I had ever experienced was boiling but the strength behind my avoidance succeeded *yet again* as I shoved it all forcefully down with copious amounts of weed *and* alcohol. Substances became the only way for us to stand in the same room together, interacting with each other exclusively when we were either high or drunk or both.

One day after work while I was cooking some sausages and peppers for dinner, a link hopped out of the pan and fell onto the floor where Roody sat waiting for this very opportunity. He inhaled it like a vacuum before I could even register what had happened. I can't remember exactly what was so funny about it but we found ourselves rolling around on the floor in a severe fit of the weed giggles, tears streaming down our faces.

"Isaac, I love you when you're high," I giggled between gasps of air, playfully batting Roody's nose away from my face.

SNAP!

The last piece of our relationship slipped into place, completing the mental partnership puzzle I'd been working so hard to avoid finishing. I had lied. A word was missing from that sentence. A word that would have exposed the truth aloud.

Isaac, I ONLY love you when you're high, I thought, correcting myself.

I only love myself when I'm high.

The gravity of that acknowledgment sobered me quickly, grounding my thoughts in the truth of my reality. This wasn't the love I wanted, this was codependency and as I looked over the side of the life raft and into the waters of my nightmares that night, I saw the long shadow of the serpent in the depths. The fear of being discovered echoed across imaginary seas, threatening to pull me under the waves.

My secrets were ready to come out but I didn't know if I was ready for *them*.

Between the acknowledgment of my situation and the amplification of my nightmares I knew it was time to seek help and, most importantly, I knew that I needed to try. I googled "therapists near me" the next morning and scheduled an appointment with the first woman who looked remotely trustworthy. I told myself that credit cards existed for a reason.

It wasn't long before the friction of our substance-infused evenings together exceeded each of our limits. Caught between the intentional avoidance of our inevitable separation and the everyday dissonance in our relationship, something had to give. Isaac hit the pressure release valve first and took a job five hours south in Oregon. The pay was significantly higher but he had to live onsite. As much as I protested, I felt an internal sense of relief paired with guilt and loathing for my own cowardice. We both stubbornly refused to acknowledge the implications of this physical separation, telling each other that we'd done long-distance before and we could do it again.

While he was away I began working with my new therapist and finally felt safe enough to confront the one thing I'd been aware of this whole time. I confessed to her that I had sexually abused my brother when I was six and he was four. It was the first time in my life I had ever said that out loud to another human being. With the resonance of my vocal chords, the words of my confession solidified the memories into reality. An unfathomably deep echo of pain erupted from the hole in my chest and I found myself bawling my eyes out across from a therapist I had just met two months ago. It was agony. Somehow the therapist helped me to calm down and then activated my deepest root with a sentence I'll never forget.

"Megan," she said, "what you just described to me, children don't just know how to do that—they learn it somewhere."

It resonated with truth.

What I had done was not a basic childhood curiosity about private parts, my actions at six years old were those of an adult and I knew it. Everything suddenly, horrifyingly, became clear and I knew, *I knew*, that it was true. Someone I loved long ago had done something unspeakable to me. And a part of me had known it the whole time. The therapist helped me package everything up as best we could for our next session ("containering" is the name of the technique) and I slowly walked out to my car and drove home.

That night and for many nights that followed, the leviathan threw me out of my life raft and tossed me into the sea again and again. It took everything I had to keep my head up and lungs clear. Roody became the knight in shining armor I'd been searching for all along, snuggling up with me at the end of each day and asking for long walks on the rocky beach with his one derpy eyebrow.

He lovingly demanded that I pull myself out of the depths to care for him and I happily obliged because it was easier to live for him than it was for myself. I was trying to find a way forward with the knowing but it was getting harder and harder to trudge on.

The heat of summer dried up the last of my distant relationship with Isaac. Unable to leave work, he asked me to drive down to Oregon for the weekend. We spent the night together, trying one last time to pretend it could work before he finally did us both the favor. For the life of me I can't remember the exact words he used, but he conveyed that he had never actually wanted to move to Seattle in the first place, he didn't know what to make of life anymore, and he felt a deep, soul-squeezing exhaustion in our relationship—we needed to go our separate ways.

I felt a weight lift off my shoulders as the illusion crumbled before me into the cascading depths of loss. A part of me truly did love him but I also knew that this was not the love I wanted. There was no anger in that moment, just the understanding that we were finally at the end of the road and a sadness that transcended the time we'd known each other. Roody lay curled up in the front seat as I drove back, licking my hand whenever I reached over to pet him, confirming that everything was real but that he was here with me through it.

Eventually, I allowed myself to feel anger and donned the victim's mask as I cut the lease I could no longer afford and took out a loan to purchase a trailer. Working for the State Parks had some benefits and I was allowed to park my trailer in a maintenance host spot, paying almost nothing for the space and utilities. My purchase had been a calculated decision and would pay itself off in less than nine months with my current income—I was about to be debt-free. But another round of government interference punched me in the gut as the state's budget cuts rolled out and my position wasn't renewed for the season.

In less than three months I had verbalized one of my deepest wounds, come face-to-face with the leviathan in my nightmares, reached the end of a four-and-a-half-year relationship, lost my job, and had taken on a loan I could no longer pay.

My inner victim became cruel, lashing out at anyone and everyone until finally the only person left to hurt was me.

The world was holding its breath. Hazy, humid air brought the typical birdsong to a hushed still as I pulled on my uniform and tucked Roody into his blanket on the couch, pushing the omnipresent tidal wave of my nightmares back.

It was a quiet day but a painful one. In and out, under and over, the darkness threatened to submerge me. Intrusive thoughts stabbed me again and again, spilling my guts across the floor and showing me everything I didn't want to see. The office began to close in, my throat tightened and clenched as the leviathan squeezed my body beneath the waves. I struggled for breath as the compression exceeded my limits, expelling any last bits of air from my body in a panic.

DING!

The corners of my mouth shot up as a lifetime of conditioning took over, spreading the most authentic smile it could muster across my face. The park had a visitor. They'd come from Tacoma for the day after seeing Dash Point pop up in a Google search.

"I've lived here for forty years and never knew this place existed!" they smiled. "I live so close... you'd've thought I'd've heard about it by now, but nope! I bet it's a little hidden gem. What trails would you recommend?"

I pulled out a map and began circling features with a red marker, completely operating from habit. But with my autopilot fully engaged the panic found space to simmer again. The smile plastered across my face began to ache and I desperately prayed for them to leave before the facade crumbled away.

Thankfully, blessedly, magnificently, they wrapped up their words and waved back at me as they walked out the door.

Silence loomed in their wake.

The leviathan, taking advantage of the opening in my defenses, consumed me. I ran back to the bathroom, chest heaving, clawing my way to the surface until my breathing slowed and I was able to return to my place behind the front desk. This scenario repeated itself several times. Finally, the sun sank beneath the trees and darkness crept into every corner of my world. My shift was over.

I locked up the office, walked back across the gravel road, and tried to give everything I had left to Roody-Roo. He had never asked to be shoved in a small trailer all day with only a short walk or two to relieve himself. He deserved better than me.

The slow, dripping ichor of guilt oozed out of the hole in my heart and wove through the suffocating depths of my personal hell. I pulled up *That 70's Show* on my laptop, hoping that some background noise would stem the inevitable but something was different today. Today wasn't just a battle, it was the height of the war and though I knew what lay ahead, here at the very end of the road, I still clung to my tattered cloak of avoidance until I slipped over the edge of oblivion.

I don't remember how it got there but the weight of the Smith & Wesson compact in my palm was undeniable. I mechanically loaded the chamber with a single bullet—no need for a magazine, I had a steady hand—and held it under my chin. Tears streamed down my face in silence as I asked myself the only question that made any sense.

Which direction should I point this to limit the mess?

Someone would need to clean this up.

Keep your finger straight and off the trigger—the Marine Corps mantra I'd embodied since holding my first M16 in boot camp no longer applied. I took one last breath.

Suddenly, little Roody-Roo was vomiting all over the floor at my feet.

I looked down at him in shock, watching his stomach heave a few more times before empathy snapped me back into reality. I felt so awful and guilty for what he had been about to experience that I dropped the gun on the bed and bent down to care for him without a second thought. He crawled into my lap as I finished cleaning his mess, love emanating from every fiber of his being, and I knew, somewhere deep within me, that I had won. He loved me not for what I could do or produce or give away, he loved me simply because I loved him and I still had some love within me.

I picked up the phone and called for help.

A few weeks later I sold my trailer, tightened down the ratchet straps covering a tarp in the bed of my truck, and pulled out onto the road. I was headed to Minnesota to live with a veteran friend and her family who had offered me room and board until I got back on my feet. It was a humbling moment, one of many that would follow, but I had finally decided to throw all my cards in this basket called life and humbling moments are a part of the deal.

I looked over at the empty passenger seat and teared up. Roody was staying in Seattle with his new owners, a couple who had been trying unsuccessfully for kids and just wanted a little dude to share their love with. It was one of the hardest decisions I've ever made but I couldn't promise him I'd stay alive. I was just trying to make it one day at a time and he deserved a life with people who were fully present.

The sun was setting as I drove out the east side of the Cascades. There was no agenda, no job to race off to, no people to take care of, just me, myself and I. So when I saw a sign for a scenic view I pulled off I-90 to check it out on a whim. After hiking up a loose gravel trail I found myself looking at the metal sculptures of Washington's Wild Horse Monument and gazing out at the most beautiful sunset I have ever seen. The warm, evening light fell across my face as I looked back towards the mountains. I had unearthed much over the last several years, willingly or not, and now sat upon my first big hill of acknowledgment.

Gazing down into the valley below, I saw the shadows of the leviathan and the demons of my nightmares waiting for me. There wasn't any sense of urgency and though I still felt fear at the concept of knowing, I knew that the only way out was through. My nightmares had been waiting for this moment ever since I was six years old. They had never given up on me. They knew I had the strength to see my own truth, to see *them*, and they were ready to show me what I needed to know—together. My nightmares were there to help me grieve the loss of a young girl, and that girl was me.

7

Right Time, Right Place

Slowly, my eyes adjusted to the darkness of this borrowed bedroom. Light from the streetlamp on the corner filtered through the blinds in chunky slats of orange, illuminating the child-sized desk along the wall to my right and a blue glow emanating from the space under the door—the nightlight in the bathroom across the hall. But something about the blue and orange light was strange. It shimmered in a way, like that black hole from *Interstellar*, as if it were being sucked into a void. A feeling of deep unease triggered the ever-present panic in my mind. My breath quickened and became shallow. Each inhale took conscious effort. I tried to shift around but my body was completely frozen. My arms were locked into place, my fingers and toes lay slack incapable of even a small wiggle, and I discovered that even my mouth was paralyzed as I tried to call for help.

Adrenaline began coursing through my limbs. Not yet comprehending that this was a dream, I began frantically searching for whoever it was that had drugged me. I slid my gaze quickly from the desk to the door—still closed—and from the door to the corner. Nothing. The bookshelf hadn't changed, there was nothing at the foot of my bed... wait! There! There in the left corner of the ceiling was a dark mass. It was nothing more than a wispy black cloud at first but slowly and with unearthly fluidity, it solidified into a figure. It clung to the ceiling with spider-like precision and its face rested at an unnatural angle, assisted by a collection of unnerving, visibly mutated ligaments. The more I tried to focus, the more it solidified. The creature waved its long, spindly appendages as it summoned a cloak out of midair. Wrapping its body in dripping black robes it turned to look at me but where its face should have been was nothing more than a yawning hole. Somehow, this was more terrifying than anything I had ever encountered before. A bloodcurdling scream erupted from the depths of my soul but was unable to release itself past my frozen, clenched teeth and into the physical world, reverberating through my body in wave after wave of amplified terror.

I watched as the creature gingerly made its way toward me, taking its time to revel in the fear perspiring from my skin before slowly gliding to a stop at the foot of my bed. It had shapeshifted in that short span of time, donning the figure of a woman from its macabre repertoire. Her inky robes were embroidered with old, intricate lacework and a thin veil descended over the void of her face, like a mourning widow. I felt her cruel smile without needing to see it and *knew*, beyond a doubt, that she was both my beginning and my end.

SNAP!

Adrenaline overrode the paralysis, propelling me upright as I gasped for air. The woman was gone.

It was just a nightmare, I repeated to myself. *It was just a nightmare.* But deep down I knew it wasn't just a nightmare. The figure on the ceiling, the woman at the foot of my bed, was real. I knew she didn't exist in the waking world but *she was real*. She felt familiar.

I turned on the lamp, lightly punched my legs to get the circulation going and slowly, with conscious awareness, placed both feet on the floor—a grounding technique I'd started recently—before walking to the kitchen to start a pot of coffee. The sun hadn't risen yet but I knew I couldn't fall back asleep. I grabbed the journal I'd recently purchased and opened it to a blank page, writing down this most recent episode of sleep paralysis. Once I had finished, I wrapped my hands around the warm mug, grounding further through the sensation of its heat and the smell of roasted beans, and stared at what I had written while trying to make sense of it.

Was the woman a part of myself representing my deepest fear? Was she an ancestor trying to make her traumas known because her energy had passed through our shared DNA? Or had she really been someone I knew, a remnant of the echo I didn't want to look at? Most importantly, what was she doing in my nightmare?

The questions were endless.

(Exploration and Interpretation, Sleep Paralysis)

Everyone has a right time and a right place to begin exploring and healing their nightmares. The word *right* does not mean perfect nor does it mean easy, the word *right* simply means *acceptable*. Before my near demise in Seattle I had spent the majority of my life in the pit of deep, suicidal depression, neither here nor there on the "let's try to live" front, but as soon as I put the gun down I stepped out of that liminal space and onto the path that had been waiting for me. I realized that I did, in fact, want to live and that I was willing to try even after knowing the gist of what I had experienced as a child. In Minnesota, I realized that I had found the right time of my life and the right environment for me to explore healing and working with my nightmares and I continued to move in the direction of rightness over the years that followed.

There are many ways to find yourself in the right time to work with your nightmares. For some, it's as simple as waking up and choosing to finally take a conscious step forward into their lives or to show up for themselves with awareness. For others it might be finally accepting the offered help of their friends and family, deciding to give up a bad habit like smoking, or even opening up a conversation with someone that they've had a difficult history with. It doesn't have to be nearly as dramatic as choosing to live but the fact is that there's *always* a choice involved.

Your right time begins when you consciously choose yourself.

Working in tandem with right time is the concept of right place which is not just a physical location. Right place refers to the totality of your environment including friends, family, housing situation, job, and the general timbre of your day-to-day life. My childhood environment was painful and unsafe. Not only did I experience psychological, physical, and sexual traumas through- out its duration, but I was specifically told and guilted into not making those traumas a big deal. If I had tried to crack open my nightmares (both the ones I experienced in dreamtime and the ones I lived through) while in that environment, I would not have had the tools, knowledge, nor the support necessary to help me through the process and it could have done more harm than good. My childhood home was not the right place to support my healing.

My early-adult environment wasn't much better as I spent most of my energy on the duties I held in the military, the psychological stamina needed for my job, and the extra work I took on to unconsciously fill the remaining space. I intentionally avoided myself. Additionally, I was still in that relationship with Isaac which mimicked the codependency I had grown up with. I thought he needed me and that the only value I had as an individual was what I could do for others. I did not yet have a sense of inherent worth. It should be noted that just because it wasn't the right place doesn't mean it wasn't helpful. My military experience launched me into the realm of self-exploration and Isaac helped me identify what sort of love I truly wanted in my life—two necessary things that directly led me onto the path of healing.

In that context, it makes sense now that I found my right place in Minnesota. Not only did the physical location feel good but I was surrounded by a new set of people—people that were actively trying to better their lives and focus on their wellbeing. I developed new, healthy friendships that weren't rooted in collective, drunken avoidance, found jobs that actually resonated with me and gave me something to look forward to, and began carving out time to intentionally have fun and participate in hobbies that brought me joy again. Right place is a combination of things: a physical location that feels good, a supportive social and/or familial environment, and work that resonates with you or at least provides time well-spent.

Finding my right place didn't happen overnight though, it took about a year for me to really stick the landing and there were many different people, jobs, and homes that came into and left my life during that time as I tried to find the *right* (acceptable) combination. It was like playing *Castles of Burgundy* (one of my favorite resource-building board games); it requires effort and concentration but the more you play it, the more you understand what resources you instinctively tend to gather, the strengths that you naturally have, and the niche you want to carve out in the game. It's entirely what you make of it.

Within the first fourteen months of moving to Minnesota, I lived in five different homes. At first I was with my military friends and their four kids whom I adored in a suburb of the Twin Cities. Back in Maryland I babysat for them relatively often and had fond memories of holding two of their kids as babies and singing them to sleep so it was with a beautiful sense of nostalgia that I got to be a part of their lives again. My friends showed me a kindness I'd never known before. They not only let me sleep in a spare room for a few months but covered my food as well in exchange for help with their kids. While living with them, I met some of their friends and relatives at weekly board game nights and quickly developed several new friendships (including one with my future husband, Brandon). We'd tuck the kids into bed, crack open some beers and beat the shit out of each other in *Ticket to Ride* or laugh until we cried through three rounds of *Monikers*. It felt good to be happy again.

Between board game nights and playing with the kids I interviewed for several jobs and got an offer to start working as the administrative assistant for a small real estate photography company. Within two months I had saved up some money and started looking for a room to rent on my own. I loved their family and the kids but... four kids is a lot and I needed some space.

I found some roommates on Craigslist. Yes, *that* Craigslist and, no, they weren't creepy or weird (relatively speaking). They had a small bedroom on the second floor of a big, new house in Brooklyn Center that had just become available. After an interview at a Caribou Coffee with all four of them (I promised my friends I'd text them every 15 minutes just in case I ended up in someone's trunk) we decided that we all got along well enough so I moved in a week later for $400/month which I'd pay them via Venmo.

My new roommates were from every walk of life. In the room across the hall from me was a local comedian, living in the small room downstairs was a guy who worked for a big medical device company, and in the larger room across from him was a couple who traveled often to visit their family in South America. We shared the kitchen, dining room, den, and dance studio (they had covered the walls of the main living room in floor-to-ceiling mirrors but I swear they weren't weird). We were all cleanliness-oriented people and made sure to tell each other when we were having guests over so there were no surprises. It was exactly what I needed.

While living in Brooklyn Center, my new friend Brandon and I found ourselves hanging out more often and began to dance the romantic tension tango. I really, *really* enjoyed Brandon's company. He was a total nerd and though I had previously told my friends that I was, "utterly, profoundly and completely done with men," they continued to invite him over anyways. The minute he started talking about his Magic the Gathering tournaments my heart melted, but my ex and I had split less than a year ago and I got caught up in the *has it been long enough?* line of mental questioning. I was pushing against old, outdated beliefs in my head and held myself back from what I intrinsically knew I wanted:

Brandon. Today, I believe that there isn't any particular length of time that makes it acceptable to move on, love is love and it's about finding *your* right time.

One night after his roommates had gone to bed we found ourselves alone watching the very bloody end of *Ninja Assassin* and started scooting closer together. As the movie ended the tension grew. Neither of us wanted me to leave so Brandon asked if I wanted to head up to his room to watch another movie—his favorite, *Gladiator*. Yes. Yes, I absolutely wanted to watch that movie... with Brandon... in his room *upstairs*. It wasn't long before things got heated. I knew we both wanted more but in an attempt over the last year to avoid sexual attraction and stick to the narrative that I was "done with men" I had specifically grown out my leg hair as a personal deterrent.

Fuck, I thought, remembering that my legs now looked like they belonged to Sasquatch. My brain started to get a little panicky until a random thought popped into my head: *just fuck it.*

Yeah, I nodded internally, *fuck it!* Heeding that thought both figuratively and soon to be literally, I pulled back and looked at him with a seriousness in my eyes (somehow I'd landed in his lap), if this was ever going to become something else I wanted to start this potential relationship with honesty even if it seemed absolutely ridiculous and even if I was embarrassed. I was here on this earth to live now so I was going to fucking *live*.

"I want to have sex but only if you do and... if you do, there's something I have to tell you." *Oh God, Meg, that makes it sound like you have a fucking STD!* I shouted in my head.

He paused for a second before responding. "I want that too but only if you're comfortable," he replied. "I'll never push you. What is it?"

"I have Chewbacca legs."

The look on his face was a cross between true confusion and barely contained hysterical laughter. I couldn't help it, my face screwed up and I descended into a fit of the giggles.

"Well," he laughed, "your legs can't be any hairier than mine! Want to see?!"

That's all I needed.

A while later I told him I needed to get home. I didn't really want to leave but it seemed too soon to stay the night. Years later, I'd find out that it would've been ok if I had stayed because he'd wanted that as well.

The first time I had Brandon over to my place on an official date he called me to say he'd be late. He was stuck behind one of the longest trains he'd ever seen and there wasn't really a way around it. I laughed at his irritation as I listened to the rumble of freight cars in the background of the receiver but really appreciated his phone call to let me know. He pulled up a while later and we made fancy grilled cheeses with gouda, cheddar, brie, bacon, avocado, and a non-Campbell's super fancy tomato soup (sorry, Campbell's). After we'd finished eating and washed the dishes we talked our ears off and moved to the den to watch a movie before talking some more.

I had never met a man like him before. Not only was he sweet and nerdy, he was also openly empathetic, genuine, funny, and we could have those deep philosophical conversations about the universe while respecting each other's ideas. Not once did I ever feel like I needed a hit or a drink just to be around him. He made me feel completely and totally safe. I felt myself starting to fall in love.

Life was getting on. My nightmares were still present and numerous and I continued recording them. There were a few recurring themes that started showing themselves in a variety of scenarios:

1. Being chased by something dangerous like a mob of bloodthirsty people, a crocodile, or even sometimes a coven of witches again, resembling my childhood nightmares.

2. A deep feeling of shame and self-loathing, where I'd find myself telling the truth or confessing something to a group of people who would then tell me how awful of a person I was.

3. A deep sense of guilt. In these nightmares, I'd be doing horrible things like accidentally hurting or killing someone when I didn't mean to. A crowd of people would always witness it and I'd end up pleading guilty to the crowd, feeling beyond horrible for what I had done.

(*Exploration and Interpretation, Recurring Themes in Minnesota*)

Though I was intrigued by the formulating knowledge of my nightmare's themes, I was more interested in all the newness of my life. *Can it really be this good? Is this what life is really like when people try to live?* I thought. I was finding out more and more of what my right place would entail though I didn't yet know that's what I was doing at the time.

I began living life intuitively and the pace of change picked up. After only five months of work I started looking for a new job. The photography company had become inundated with requests as spring turned to summer and I was juggling more hats than I had limbs available to juggle with. I felt that I wasn't getting paid enough for what I was being asked to do and my blood pressure was through the roof. I could have pushed through for the security of just having a job but I felt called to move on. After interviewing on the side with a few other companies I was quickly hired by a group called GoKart Labs who (to my slight disappointment) didn't make go-karts. A week after accepting that position, the couple who lived in the basement of our shared home in Brooklyn Center broke up and informed the rest of us that they wouldn't be renewing the lease which was set to expire in two weeks. It hit me like one of the freight trains Brandon always got stuck behind and I had no choice but to light the beacons of Gondor and call on my new friends for aid. Fortunately, a friend of a friend had another recently-vacated room open for rent and I moved that same week to live with my new acquaintances just ten minutes south. Their house came with the best perk I could have asked for: a gray, oversized mop of a dog who loved belly rubs named Bernie. The rent was a little more expensive, but their home was right on a bus route that could drop me off a block from my new job. I took a deep breath and made it through all of the change life had just thrown at me.

It was easy to settle into my new job because I loved it. GoKart Labs was a tech start-up that helped update older businesses to the newness of the online space. They designed new websites, apps, and made old companies (like financial and medical institutions) more accessible for people with disabilities. Everyone liked what they did and GoKart had one of the most supportive environments I've ever had the pleasure of working in. Seriously. They were conscientious, fun, efficient, and meaningful. We all supported each other. It was kind of weird at first until I realized I didn't have to wait for the ball to drop because there wasn't a ball *to* drop and I could actually see myself working there long term. I didn't have a crazy interesting or high-paying job—I was an administrative assistant—but the environment was worth it and I did enjoy being a jack-of-all-trades who could find a way to organize, fix, or resolve any issue. As a bonus, they let me book the big conference room after hours for the new D&D campaign I started! At the end of each Friday some coworkers and I would grab a brew from the office beer fridge (it was that kind of place) and throw dice. Sometimes I'd pinch myself just to make sure it wasn't all a dream.

With a more comfortable job and a new place to stay, I continued understanding more of my nightmares. The cloaked woman kept visiting me in episodes of sleep paralysis and while I hadn't made any progress in picking her specific meaning apart, I felt a lot of things start to shift in my "regular" nightmares with their emotional themes. I began to feel like I needed to confess part of my life to Brandon. I needed him to know what he was getting into with me because if it was too much (and I was sure that it was) I didn't want to get too attached before it inevitably ended. I pulled out my serious face and explained to him that if we were going to keep dating he needed to know that I had major depression, anxiety, experienced panic attacks, and had almost committed suicide before coming here to Minnesota. It felt like dropping a bombshell. I told him that I was a work in progress but, good news, I was an *aware* work in progress! Huzzah! I held my breath, fearing the worst, but he didn't even hesitate before speaking, stating that he already knew some of those things and he was very glad that I had lived to meet him. I kept asking if all of that was ok, seeking reassurance that he had, indeed, comprehended what I'd said because every person I had ever loved before had told me I was too much. He *did* understand and while he was glad that I told him, his feelings hadn't changed.

Brandon was the first person who acknowledged my experience without judgment *on the spot*. He didn't try to fix me. He didn't make it a big deal—he waited for me to show him what kind of a deal it was. Brandon also intrinsically understood that he wasn't responsible for my thoughts and feelings. As my boyfriend, he wanted to support me in healing myself. Suddenly, honesty wasn't so bad.

Our relationship continued to grow and, at the same time, my work at Go-Kart was becoming more fulfilling, but my new roommates had started to shift. Unbeknownst to the friend who had connected us, one of them "forgot" to disclose that they had a severe case of bipolar disorder combined with extremely high anxiety, outbursts of violence, and they frequently forgot to take their meditation. At first, I didn't think anything of it but the missed medications started to affect my roommate more and more until one morning I heard glass shattering in their bedroom. They had tried to take a nap while their partner was at work and it was a day they forgot to take their meds. I opened the door and found them sleepwalking while holding a lamp with the shade torn off and a half-smashed lightbulb protruding from the stand. I didn't know what to do and before I could think, they somehow sensed my presence in their sleep and leapt across the room to where I was standing in the doorway. I quickly tried to shut it but they got their foot in the crack and started lashing out at me. I know they didn't mean to do it but their home wasn't safe for me anymore and I started locking my bedroom door at night just in case.

I found another new place with yet another friend of a friend who also, suddenly, had a vacant room. (Do you see a pattern here? In the language of the universe I was looking to fill open spaces just like I was trying to fill in the blank memory spaces my nightmares were trying to show me.)

Jade was an ex-Mormon I had just met that year and there was some weird falling out between her and some of our mutual friends but I needed a place to live and she had one. Like I had with my other ex-Mormon friend, Cannon, in the military, Jade and I laughed through her many tales of experiences in the LDS which included topics like wearing their special full-body underwear (because if your nipples were left exposed the devil could tease them), the details of how dinosaur bones weren't really from Earth since they crashed here on an asteroid, and how much income one had to tithe to the church to retain their status. Really, we just enjoyed sharing stories of our most ridiculous and traumatic moments.

It was in this fourth home that I began to really pick up on the animosity that was growing amongst my friends. Several months earlier my military friends had a falling out with Brandon's roommates. The "he said, she said, they said" argument drew out and got ugly. Brandon and I tried suggesting that they talk it out but it became a sticking point and the wedge drove itself deeper. My military friends refused to let it go or to even try to resolve it and every time Brandon and I hung out with them they would verbally shit all over his roommates. It was awful. I asked my military friends to drop it when we were with them but it was like they were incapable of talking about anything else. They fixated every ounce of their energy on the drama and reveled in it. On the other hand, Brandon's roommates wanted to move on and when we asked that they not bring it up or make it a focal point of our evening they understood. They respected our ask and the fact that sometimes you have friends your other friends don't want to interact with and that's ok.

In the end, everyone showed their true faces and we found ourselves distanced from my military friends. It all sounds really cliche but it truly happened and through it I learned that my peace is worth protecting. Brandon's roommates rarely brought the fallout up and we enjoyed a friendship that wasn't rooted in drama and malice. They were able to let it go (at least from what I saw) even if the whole thing sucked. Those were the people we wanted in our lives—people who were willing to take what life gave them, move on, and find peace.

But there was a lot of tension between Jade and I after that. She had decided to dig her feet into the drama and our shared apartment ballooned with a bristling feeling. I once again started looking for new places to live. As autumn dipped into winter Brandon started looking to purchase a starter home and asked me to come along for my opinion. I didn't want to assume we'd move in together but after several tours and no mention of me moving or not, I asked if he just wanted my opinion because he wanted to know what *I* liked or if he wanted me to help him find *his* place. He looked at me surprised and said, "Of course I want you to search *with* me! You're moving here too, wherever *here* will be!" To him, it wasn't even a question. We laughed and agreed to state even the most obvious things to each other in the future for clarity. There wasn't a space for me to fill in this time, there was a space with my name already on it.

It was a little over a year since I had first arrived in Minnesota when we moved into a new townhome in Lino Lakes that was all our own. It was the perfect house for us at the time, sitting a block away from a trailhead and just off a main highway that led to Minneapolis. We had two big bedrooms upstairs, a big open living area on the main floor, a small office with a two-car garage in the basement and we enjoyed decorating our new home with *Star Wars* artwork and newly potted plants. Every time I looked around our home I almost couldn't believe where I was. In such a short time I had completely stepped into another life. I had formed new friendships (even though I moved on from some), found a steady, reliable job, and met a man that I not only loved deeply but who wanted to intentionally continue building a healthy relationship.

I had finally found my right time and right place.

When you choose to start showing up for yourself and acknowledge your true needs you enter your right time. When you begin to approach your life as a quest seeking what lifts you up instead of what tears you down you enter your right place. There is no right or wrong way to seek the path forward and everyone's avenue is a direct reflection of the unique choices and experiences that have created their reality thus far.

Your right time and right place do not have to look anything like mine. In Seattle, I knew that I couldn't go back to Iowa or to my parents because I'd only submerge myself back into the primordial soup that had created my dissonance in the first place so I did the hard thing and stepped out of my comfort zone—I changed. That single choice, to change myself and my environment, waterfalled into a series of alterations that led me to an entirely new state, a new way of looking and trying at life, more fulfilling work, a supportive community, and so much more.

I didn't always get it right on the first try, but through these changes, I realized there were two different types of people in my life: those who were excited and happy for me as I changed and those who were affronted by it. I took on the role of an observer once more and allowed my friends and family to show me who they truly were through their words and actions. I chose to believe them at face value.

The people who are excited for the changes you make are usually the most supportive and loving individuals. The people who are upset or angry that you're changing are afraid of change themselves because when you show them that change is possible it calls into question their own areas of dissonance and desire to change. When you change, the people around you show you what they do and do not fear and when you're trying to confront your deepest fears—your nightmares—it's ideal to surround yourself with people who support you in doing so, with people who aren't afraid of change.

It's hard to step away from people we've loved or befriended in the past, it's hard to get up and move, it's hard to learn to trust again but if you never try to step into what you need or protect your peace, then you may never find out for yourself *how good it actually can be.* That's what this is really all about. Working with nightmares, healing your experiences, *surviving...* it's all about seeking and enacting change to better your life. At the end of the day, you can't force other people to change, they have to do that themselves. All you can do is acknowledge where *you* need to change and take action.

Change is difficult by design—it was literally life or death for me—but change is at the heart of healing. Change gives us the opportunity to pick *ourselves* up and to show ourselves how resilient and strong we are. When you look around you, when you see every facet of your life, ask yourself what needs to change. Start there, take the baby steps (or giant leaps if that's more your jam), don't be afraid to ask for help and, above all, choose to live for *you.*

8
The Great Emptying

Sometimes stepping into the right time and right place can feel like moving backwards which is exactly what I experienced after moving in with Brandon in 2019. Underneath the surface I *knew* that I was finding my feet in this new way of living, progressing forward into the unexplored tunnel of my nightmares and acknowledging my demons but the intensity of it all felt overwhelming. My internal dissonance (the conflict between wanting to heal and still feeling pain) began to express itself through little things like a sudden onset of moodiness or bursting into tears for no apparent reason but, over time, my symptoms became more extreme. I found myself frequently recovering from an onslaught of three to four panic attacks a week with the intensity of those attacks increasing. In some of the more extreme episodes of panic I'd almost revert to a much younger version of myself where, as a full-ass grown woman, I would crawl under the safety of our solid oak kitchen table and hold my knees up to my chest in a protective ball, rocking back and forth between gasps of air and speaking like I was six years old again. I had a lot of shame around it but those moments were so completely consuming that all I could do was just try and make it through them. Brandon would crouch down and talk to me softly, speaking reassurances, until the episode would pass. So much for being a Marine Corps veteran.

At this stage, I had been intentionally observing my nightmares for about a year and a half. Acknowledging them was the most important thing at this point and their recurring themes had begun to show me what I needed to work with. I put effort into trying to remember them more often, building my recall ability through habit-forming processes. The more I tried to recall and write down my nightmares, the more my brain understood that I valued this information. I'd wake, recall, record, and read through my nightmares one after the other. I didn't fully understand what they were showing me at first but the more I tried to comprehend what I was telling myself through their imagery and emotion, the more I understood that they were all showing me what I feared. I was afraid of the truth catching up to me (the truth of who, exactly, had sexually abused me), I was afraid of everyone learning what I had done to my brother and hating me for it, and I was afraid of feeling so guilty that I'd want to kill myself again. I was afraid of feeling all of the things that were already there. Somehow, I intuitively knew *feeling* was exactly what I needed to do. I needed to feel my way through the fear. I needed to feel it so that I could finally clear it from my system and be free.

Today, I know that not everyone needs this, but I did. I specify that it was necessary for me because there's no one right way to move through any of our shit, there's only the way that *you* need in the right time and the right place for you. For me, the safety and security of a healthy partnership, healthy friendships, a healthy work environment, and the first steady place to call home I'd had in years signaled to my whole system that it was finally safe to explore my shit. Every moment of my existence from birth onward where I had suppressed the urge to panic, cry, tear myself apart, or emotionally explode had been stored away somewhere in my mind-body-energy system and it was all ready to go.

So began the time of the great emptying.

Have you ever heard that phrase, "It has to get worse before it gets better?" Well that's what I stepped into and I knew it would have to get worse because the only way for me to move forward was to go back and sit with my child self and experience her. This was a part of my process. She came out in panic attacks mostly but I also started hurting myself again like I had when I was younger by punching the tops of my legs until they bruised or pinching myself so hard that I cried. I was trying to figure out how to release all of the pain while continuing to *want* to live and, somehow, the physicality of it made me feel like I wasn't going crazy. It told me this was real.

Brandon was incredibly supportive through all of this, innately knowing when to talk to me and when to just be in space with me. He never tried to fix me, understanding that only *I* could really work this out, and when I broke down in the I'm-so-sorries after each panic attack he was there to hold me with his comforting presence, calmly imparting that there was no need for the sorries because *I* was the one in pain and suffering and this was part of the release process.

Of course, our relationship wasn't perfect, we argued and said unkind things to each other as many partners do, but every night before we went to bed we made sure to talk through our problems and clear the slate for the next day before Brandon would wrap me up like a burrito in the sheets and kiss me goodnight (yes, he really is that sweet and yes, he still does this). It was that willingness on both of our accounts—to unequivocally be honest with each other and let go of the need to be right, replacing it with the need to be human—that supported me the most. But I knew that no matter how good Brandon was at being there for me, it was my responsibility to heal myself and that I probably needed help from a psychological professional.

Living with someone who has a mental illness or who has experienced trauma is not easy and I saw the toll it was taking on him. Instead of picking away at our relationship, it made me want to help myself even more in order to move through it all to emerge on the other side where *both* of us were healed, healthy, and able to explore our relationship without traumatic memories getting in the way. Healthy love, friendship, and support can be incredibly beneficial to the healing experience but with the intensity of my traumas, I knew that I needed solid, psychological tools and technical knowledge to guide me along the way. I once again googled "therapists in my area" and soon had an appointment booked with Rachel whose office was just five minutes away.

Rachel is the therapist who changed my life. All of my therapists have been helpful even if I only went to a single session, but Rachel was the one I resonated with the most, and when you find a therapist or other healer that you resonate with it's so much easier to share your story and unique needs. In the beginning, the part of me that self-sabotages resulted in a skipped session here or there but as soon as I began applying myself to our sessions I began looking forward to our time together. I allowed myself to step into the flow. Over the next couple of years, I opened up and tried anything she suggested in an attempt to continue moving forward and clear out the shit. We explored Internal Family Systems (IFS), parts work, Eye Movement Desensitization and Processing (EMDR), Cognitive Behavioral Therapy (CBT), enneagram, and, most importantly, my nightmares. A large part of my healing experience was allowing myself to try different techniques and build a toolbox for emotional regulation and management—like *actually* trying techniques, not just saying I would do it and then never following through. I put effort into myself and the more I tried, the more I interrupted my former habits, continued to actively change for the better, disrupted and reworked my neurological pathways, and found what works best for me.

At the same time, I was recalling my nightmares with more regularity and had gotten relatively good at dissecting and interpreting them. Sometimes I'd google dream meanings or look up definitions in a dream dictionary but many of the answers I found were unsatisfactory and didn't feel like they resonated. I began to understand that those interpretation resources were missing a key component: the individual dreamer's life context. Every single person on the face of the planet has their own unique symbolic language in the dreamspace which is defined by the distinctive combination of life experiences, thoughts, emotions, and beliefs of each individual. At the end of the day, it is *you* that gives meaning to your dreams.

Today, my go-to example for explaining unique symbolic language is the imagery of a dog. When you google "meaning of dog in dream" you'll most likely find sources telling you that a dog represents love or loyalty. However, I've learned that dog imagery in my personal dream language represents something that I feel strongly responsible for, as formed by my relationship with Roody-Roo.

And if someone who had been attacked by a dog in their life dreamed of one, the dog's image almost certainly wouldn't mean love or loyalty to them, it'd be an exploration of that traumatic event, or it would represent something dangerous and harmful depending on how much work they'd done to move through the memory. All these definitions about a dog can be correct depending on the individual who has dreamed them and their unique combination of life experiences. Dream dictionaries can provide us with ideas and starting points for defining imagery but this is why it's so crucial to ask what *you* think the imagery means. You and your experiences are the key elements in dream and nightmare interpretation.

As I began to learn my own unique symbolic language through the observation of my nightmares, I began to learn more about myself. I started bringing my nightmare interpretations to my sessions with Rachel. The specific emotions that expressed themselves in my nightmares (guilt and shame) showed me that I needed to work on self-forgiveness and my innate sense of worth. Sometimes specific memories would play out in my nightmares over and over again, indicating that I needed to revisit and reprocess those individual moments. I'd tell Rachel the most recent themes of my nightmares and we use them as a starting point for our sessions.

I was uncovering my individual healing pathway.

Each memory and emotion surfaced in *my* right order, walking me through a step-by-step healing process that my mind-body-energy system had designed specifically for me. I focused on being in the present moment and observing what came up on any given day, trusting that my mind would show me what I needed to know in the order that I needed to know it. Over time, Rachel and I developed a deep sense of trust—I trusted Rachel to guide me through my experience and she trusted my nightmares and me to lead the way forward one memory at a time. The more I opened up to Rachel, the more material I brought to our sessions, and the more quickly I began to move through it all. Going back to the beginning of this book, there are many healing services and methods out there, but they can only help you as much as you allow them to. It can be incredibly difficult to share your deepest, darkest shit with a person you barely know but the more you try and open up, the more you apply yourself and put effort into the process, the more those healers can help you.

As a teenager, I'd come home from high school, do my homework and chores, and then lie down in bed for the rest of the afternoon to daydream that I was in Middle Earth. I was obsessed with *The Lord of the Rings* (even going so far as to plaster a massive poster of Legolas on the ceiling directly above my bed which my cousin and I still laugh about) and, as a coping mechanism, would place myself in that imaginary world to escape the environment of my reality. Day after day I'd lie there and pretend I was somewhere else, saving a different world instead of hurting people in my own. After becoming an adult I thought back on those times with embarrassment. I was ashamed that I had "wasted away" much of my time by lying in that room. I thought that my daydreaming years had been unhealthy but through my sessions with Rachel I realized that it wasn't me that was unhealthy, it was the totality of my environment—my daydreaming was just one of the many techniques that my child-self utilized at the time to help me survive.

All of the experiences, memories, and the structure of my child-hood environment shaped me as a human being. My high school daydreams had been a way of trying to escape the overwhelming forces at home, all of my "freak out sessions" and emotional ex-plosions had been my body opening the pressure relief valve, and everything I was now experiencing as an adult was understand-able when you took my totality into context. The main difference was that now I *saw them* as coping mechanisms and not just as a personality trait which meant that I could change them and find better, healthier ways for me to move through my experiences.

As Rachel and I continued exploring the pathway of my night-mares, she introduced me to a powerful grounding technique that not only really worked for me but harnessed the old power of my imagination—the Sanctuary. Sometimes the pain of my memories would be so great that we'd need to retreat from our explorations into a mentally safe, grounded, and centered space. With Rachel's guidance, I created a protected, imaginary location somewhere in my ether that she could guide me to if the need arose. Once I had found a sense of measured balance within myself again we'd come back to reality and continue on with our session. At that point in time, for someone whose life had been so horrifyingly painful, sometimes the only truly safe-feeling spaces were imagined.

I ended up repurposing an old space that I had already built in my imagination while adventuring through Middle Earth when I was a teenager. It was a beautiful grove in Rivendell. In the extended edition of the films, there's a scene with Aragorn at his mother Gilraen's memorial. He gently, peacefully, wipes away the moss and plant growth from her features, clearing her statue with respect and love. The feeling of that place, the sorrowful but peaceful and safe resonance, called to me and it was in that grove that I created my Sanctuary. In my imagination, I planted a tree there, sat on a stone bench by the edge of a small, bubbling pond, and brought the different parts of myself to safety that were struggling through the pain. It was divinely shielded. No one could find it as it was under the protection of Elrond's magick.

After describing this place to Rachel, she could mentally walk me to the space whenever the need arose, helping me find a sense of calm again before we returned and continued our exploration. The purpose of using imaginative techniques is not to try and escape reality, it's to show us that we, as individuals, are capable of bringing safety and peace into our own lives. My Sanctuary showed me that I am a powerful healing force and that I do, in fact, have the ability to heal myself. It was like an introductory course in how to self-regulate by using the tools I innately held as a child to make it through this existence. Coping techniques and mechanisms aren't bad or wrong, they're a way of getting through traumatic moments when we don't know how else to do it. When we are finally able to see a coping mechanism for what it is, we can separate it from our identity and replace it with a much healthier experience. The shame I had for my imagination washed away every time I intentionally and with conscious intent stepped inside my Sanctuary, reclaimed a sense of balance, and walked out of it again.

"Containering" is another psychological exercise that worked well for me and, once again, it used the power of my imagination. At the end of each session Rachel would invite me to visualize myself picking up all of the pieces of my story that we'd opened and place them in a secure container for next time. The idea was that I didn't have to carry my shit out into the world and I didn't have to think about it until the next time we met. I repurposed my imaginative nature by creating a scene where I'd hold a big, clear glass jar. I'd stuff all of the blackness from our session into it like Hermione stuffing whole tents into her bottomless clutch. Then I'd hand off my jar to Captain Jack Sparrow who would prance around yelling about his jar of *diiiiirrrt!* before burying it in the sand on the beach and adding a big X to the imaginary map I held that detailed my healing pathway.

At the beginning of our next session, I'd mentally grab my map, dig up the jar of dirt, and open it again for us to continue exploring. The mental separation began to show me that it was ok to carry on with my life and even, dare I say, have fun! I didn't have to think about what I'd done to my brother or what had been done to me every waking moment of every single day. I allowed myself to leave the *diiiiirrrt* where I could find it later. There's a time and a place for healing and it's not a requirement to be fully immersed in it 24/7.

Every technique I added to my toolbox helped me progress and become more present and loving towards myself and to the people around me which is, ultimately, what I truly cared about.

As my healing work with Rachel allowed the deep wells of pain to safely emerge I began to feel a sort of bubbling in the first months of 2020. I imagine it's how the Earth feels when pressure builds in a lava chamber right before an eruption. The collective fear of the global Covid pandemic intensified my nightmares and one of them in particular punched me right in the proverbial gut.

A verbatim nightmare from my dream journal:

I don't remember how it began but at some point I was in my Oma's basement. It was dark, old, lit by only a single bulb on a chain from the ceiling, one of the creepy ones, and dirt was stuck in corners and rivets on the floor. There was a showerhead in the middle of the basement and a drain in the floor under it. Nothing else really, the rest of the basement was pretty much empty. I knew I had to take a shower there, under the lone bulb in the stream of water that had no walls, no protection from eyes or a cold breeze or the dirt swirling on the floor. I don't remember the water though, I just assume it was there.

I was terrified. I tried to take off my clothes because that's how you shower but I couldn't take them all off. Something was watching me from the top of the stairs. I couldn't tell who but something was there. I was terrified. Tears started streaming down my cheeks. I couldn't do it and I [felt] violated, humiliated, hated, loathed, disgusted by whatever was at the top of the stairs.

(Exploration and Interpretation, The Basement Shower)

I remember waking from that nightmare, recording it, and then immediately shutting it down. It felt more like a memory than a dream. The implications of that nightmare were terrifying and, for some reason, my heart felt like it was going to explode with grief whenever I thought about it. I locked it up and threw away the key, hiding it even from Rachel.

Soon after, the veiled woman in my sleep paralysis nightmares began showing me direct images and memories of my childhood. These ones I did bring to my sessions with Rachel and we worked through them one after the other. The woman was still terrifying but I knew that even though she filled my room with an over-whelming sense of fear, she was somehow helping me.

Over time she would end up closer and closer to the edge of my bed, every episode adding up like the slow thumbing through of a flip book until she started physically interacting with me in the dreamspace. At first, it was just a light tug on my feet but as the months carried on, she started trying to drag me out of my bed by my left ankle (always the left). I'd jolt awake before slipping off the edge of the bed only to find that I hadn't moved an inch and the covers were still securely in place. She was a figment of my nightmares, nothing more, but her power there was immense. Underneath it all I had the sense of knowing that I was close to a turning point and that she was trying to pull me across some unknown line into territory I had never before ventured.

The pandemic fully arrived and the world went into lockdown. Brandon and I tried having fun where we could and as spring passed into summer we found ourselves disc golfing at every op-portunity. It was the perfect pandemic activity: free and outside. But the heat and humidity of a Minnesotan summer further am-plified the feeling of accumulating pressure until my stored trauma was finally ready to blow.

One day we headed to a little thirteen-hole course in Fridley called Riverfront and chucked discs to our hearts' content before slowly walking back to the car and draining the last of our Gatorades. It had been exceptionally hot and humid and I knew I probably had a heat-related illness when the air conditioning became too cold and I got the chills on the car ride home. I immediately started taking in fluids and resting, googling all the ways to recover from heat exhaustion while trying not to snap at Brandon through some extreme irritability.

I recovered enough to feel sort of normal again and thought nothing of it. We decided to make something easy for dinner: refried bean burritos with a little cheese, hot sauce, and sour cream. It was a meal I'd eaten often as a kid when my parents were low on money and I found myself diving into the reliquary of memory with every bite. The combination of possible heat exhaustion and nostalgia started working together. Raw, emotional pain spilled over the wells of my eyes as I ate my cost-effective burrito. I ran downstairs and took a few quick draws of weed from my one-hitter to beat the memories back into submission—I didn't have the energy for a processing moment. I began to relax, played some Mario Kart with Brandon, and went to bed early.

SEARING PAIN

It was sudden and excruciating. I tried to roll over and change positions just in case it was gas but it got worse. Snapping awake I threw the covers off and hobbled into the bathroom, not sure if I needed to throw up or take a shit. Another wave of mind-numbing pain coursed through my abdomen. The sweats started pouring off of my forehead, my limbs started shaking and I got the feeling that I was about to pass out.

Fuck, I thought. *I bet this is another ruptured ovarian cyst...* (I'd had PCOS since I was a teenager and had experienced the pain of a ruptured cyst before). *Brandon might have to take me in.*

The thought that immediately followed was, *Why is my cheek on the floor?* Between the span of two thoughts I had passed out on the toilet and my face was smooshed up against the bathtub. I couldn't move, it was almost as if I were in one of my sleep paralysis nightmares except this time the lights were on and I was butt-ass naked laying on the bathroom floor. *That's what I get for sleeping in the nude*, I thought.

I lay there a little while longer, breathing through waves of extreme pain and unable to move more than my fingers and toes, before realizing that Brandon wasn't coming. If there were an Olympic sport for sleeping Brandon would earn the gold. He could stay in dreamland through the passing of a freight train. I realized that I needed to call out for him but my lips were just as numb as my limbs and all that I could muster was a pathetic, wheezing grunt. Thankfully, *blessedly*, he woke up after a few muffled cries and opened the bathroom door. It didn't take a rocket scientist to know that something was wrong so he immediately launched into a series of questions to determine if I'd hit my head on the way down or not and if he could safely move me. He asked if I needed an ambulance and I actually had the audacity to decline at first before begrudgingly whispering, *yes*.

This is the part where I want to stress that I absolutely love Brandon but he's not the best at answering medical emergencies. As I lay curled up on the floor flinching in pain I heard his voice raise an octave or two and say, "Oh... I need to sit down, I might pass out..." to which I forcefully replied, "You bttr *fuckin*... stay 'wake cuz nly one us can g' down ata time." The woman on the other end of the 911 call heard him say it too and started walking him through breathing exercises and how to take care of himself so that he could take care of me. Brandon, bless his soul, is such an empathetic person that his body physically sympathizes with any emergency, sending him into involuntary vasovagal responses no matter how inconvenient.

As Brandon recovered he was able to make it down the stairs and open the front door to let in the police officer who got there first. At this point, I was still lying naked at the base of the toilet and there wasn't much I could do about it, though I was slowly regaining movement in my limbs to some extent. The officer asked me a bunch of questions including if I'd taken any drugs and I shamelessly told him about my weed, not caring if I got in trouble because I might be literally dying and if it helped them to know... well, I had already made the decision that I was going to live and I was willing to live with any necessary consequences too. We figured it wasn't the weed though because I had been smoking the same batch for a while and had never had issues before. The officer turned to Brandon and told him to put a blanket over me until the paramedics got there which he promptly did.

The ambulance arrived and I mumbled my replies to a litany of questions while continuing to regain feeling in my body which was both a blessing and a curse as the pain increased right along with my mobility. They figured I was either experiencing a heat stroke, a ruptured ovarian cyst like I suggested, or my appendix was ready to go—all of which required a visit to the ER. We packed up and Brandon helped me wiggle on a T-shirt and shorts before they asked if I needed a stretcher. Thinking of the steep staircases in our townhouse and how tightly they'd have to strap me to the board I decided to pass on the straight jacket for as long as possible and painfully scooted my way to the bottom of the stairs one step at a time at a snail's pace until I couldn't avoid the stretcher any longer.

The EMT in the back of the ambulance introduced himself as John. He was sweet and, just like he would with a child, asked me if this was my first ride in an ambulance. It was, and, yes, I *was* excited to go lights and sirens. I smiled and giggled before recoiling in pain and almost blacking out again from the movement of my laughter. He got all the IVs going and started the prep work.

When we arrived at the hospital John rolled me into a staging area for a bit—Covid was at one of its peaks and rooms were in limited supply. Eventually they found a space for me and the nurses started taking samples of my blood and scheduled ultrasounds and a CT scan. A woman handed me a wall phone and Brandon's voice came reassuringly through the other end. He wasn't sure if they'd let him into the room because of the restrictions but he was trying what he could to get there. Then, with a wave of abdominal agony, I almost passed out *again*. Someone gave me an injection of Dilaudid and said they thought it might be an ovarian torsion before rolling me off for both a pelvic and a vaginal ultrasound.

The ultrasounds were extremely uncomfortable, putting direct pressure on the center of my pain but, good news, it wasn't an ovarian torsion nor was it a ruptured cyst (though they confirmed that I still had cysts on my ovaries). They wheeled me back to my room and put their heads together on the next thing. A little while later I heard a tiny buzzing sound to my right. Unhurriedly, I turned to look for the source and saw a bumble bee flying around the room. He was a big, fat, fluffy bumble bee, one of the super cute ones. It was 4:44 am on the wall clock. I watched him buzz around as he looked for the exit, wary of his stinger and the potential for more pain but somehow I knew he wasn't there to hurt me. I had always loved bumble bees and I had the sense of knowing that he was some sort of a sign from the universe that I was going to be ok.

The next time a nurse entered the room I told her about the bee and that she needed to keep the door open to let him outside. She immediately grew concerned, thinking that I was hallucinating, until she spotted it and we both let out a sigh of relief that he was real. She turned off the lights and left the door open in a bid to draw him out. But almost as soon as she had left I needed to get up, suddenly feeling that I was about to have explosive diarrhea—the saga continued. A kind woman wheeled me as quickly as she dared to the restroom and helped me hobble through the door. Taking a massive shit while in copious amounts of pain and trying not to pass out the whole time through it was an undertaking... but I made it.

When we got back to the room I curled up on the bed and my blood pressure immediately plummeted. Barely retaining consciousness once again, I felt someone wrap a nasal cannula around my face and was put on oxygen. They didn't know what was wrong with me but I was clearly going through it. Another nurse bent down to explain that she was putting morphine into my IV and that I was about to feel much better. I sort of did, it wasn't really a good feeling but the pain did go away and I was grateful for that. I lay back on the bed and dozed...

...until I was brutally woken by a sudden wave of nausea bubbling up like lava from the depths. I pushed the call button and as soon as the nurse rushed in with a barf bag I grabbed it and expelled the most awful-smelling liquid you can imagine. It smelled like it had come straight from my intestines and it had come out of both my mouth and my nose, obstructing the oxygen tube. I pulled the cannula off my face and asked for some tissues before I started to cry. I apologized to everyone and anyone who came near me. I was sorry that I was so disgusting, I was sorry that they had to spend their time on me and most of all I was so, so sorry for... for what? I couldn't remember but I needed them to know that I was so incredibly sorry. Brandon finally entered the room wearing a thick mask and started to comfort me even though it was too late. At this point, I was in the throes of a downward mental spiral and started panicking. It takes a lot to panic while on morphine but somehow I did it. Everyone was trying to keep me calm but no amount of painkillers could suppress the years of internal mental torture that lay behind this bizarre and incredibly painful episode of whatever this was. They decided to give me an antipsychotic drug. It worked.

Finally, I calmed down and Brandon was able to keep me in a state of relative mental balance, updating a few family members on our situation just in case we needed help. The nurses came back in at some point to see if I could drink the oral contrast needed for the CT scan. They tried to see if I could stomach some plain crackers first but my gut immediately seized up in pain, refusing anything and everything so we had to go with an injection.

The CT scan came back negative for everything. By all accounts I was perfectly healthy and nothing was wrong... except for the excruciating pain that made me pass out on the toilet at home, the fact that my blood pressure dropped and I had needed oxygen in the ER, the explosive diarrhea, the vomit that came out of my nose, and the fact that I had somehow found the strength to panic through morphine. There was nothing more they could do but wait.

Eventually, the pain subsided on its own and, after a couple hours of observation without further incident, they prescribed me some oral painkillers and nausea medication, told me to come back in if it started happening again, and suggested that I follow up with my general practitioner. Through all of the scans and tests performed over the last ten hours they hadn't found anything technically wrong with me, but we all knew that *something* had happened.

Completely drained and barely conscious, Brandon pushed me out of the ER in an old mauve wheelchair and buckled me into the passenger seat. We made it home and I slept for almost two full days waking only to eat and to use the restroom. The nausea subsided, my body began to feel normal again, and, slowly, I recovered from the intensely frightening experience that only a freak incident landing in an American emergency room can give you. I lived.

To this day, we still don't know exactly what caused the $10,000 bean burrito incident (which is how Brandon and I laugh about it now). After following up with my doctor we've pieced together what we *think* happened: I experienced an anomalous event that, combined with heat exhaustion, released a massive amount of stored trauma in my mind-body-energy system. As a victim of childhood sexual abuse, much of my trauma is associated with my lower abdomen, the area that experienced intense pain during the ER episode. The brain is a powerful thing and I believe that I psychologically and emotionally released a large chunk of the trauma that had physically manifested itself in my body over time. I see it as an energy transfer. The law of energy states that energy can neither be created nor destroyed, it can only change its form. When I was a child experiencing sexual abuse, I should have been able to let that energy go from my body through emotional expression and outward processing but, within the confines of my limiting familial closed-loop system, I had to hold onto it, storing it away at its point of origination. As I stepped into my right time and right place as an adult in Minnesota and began my work with Rachel, I had created the perfect conditions to allow me to finally release the pain of that trauma.

As a child, the energy of that trauma had entered me through the abdominal area and, as an adult, it left through my abdomen as well. My painful episode in the ER was a physical expression of the great emptying.

9
Revelation Day

Summer moved into autumn and, like the changing leaves, the canopy of my dreamspace began to shift. The frequency of my sleep paralysis episodes dramatically decreased after my ER experience to about a single episode every week (down from four episodes per week) and sometimes they'd even give me a reprieve of several weeks in a row! It felt like magick. I was lighter, happier, and healthier than I had been in a long, long time and as November arrived I finally let go of my need to know *who* it had been.

Ever since Seattle, when I had first verbalized the abuse I enacted upon my brother and acknowledged that I had also been abused, the identity of my abuser had remained elusive within my memory. I knew that they had been very close to me, that they were someone I had loved and shared wonderful memories with, but I hadn't wanted to see who it was because I knew a piece of me, the happy little girl in the good memories with that individual, would die and I wasn't ready to grieve her loss.

I tried to suppress the question for a while but it sat at the back of my brain, always churning and asking "Who?" Had it been an uncle or a neighbor? A close family friend? I knew it wasn't one of my parents (they had enacted their pain upon me in other ways) but it was someone who had been very close to me. I'd get angry at my brain for asking and wondering, mentally berating myself and shoving the questions back down whenever I became aware of them, telling myself over and over again that I didn't want to know, that I didn't *need* to know. Finally, I began to win over that nagging, questioning voice in the back of my head and a sense of inner peace began to take up the space where the hole in my chest had been. I believed that I could find resolution without knowing, and in that belief I fully let go of the need to know.

Apparently, letting go was the last thing I needed to pass the point of no return, locking myself into the final leg of my healing journey. So one November afternoon in 2020, as I was doing the dishes, I was suddenly slammed with a lifetime of repressed self-knowledge. All of my memories came back to me in an instant. They poured relentlessly in, one after another, until the unfinished puzzle that had been my brain these last two decades finally lay complete. Not only did I know exactly who had sexually abused me but I was suddenly reliving everything they had ever done. Brandon came upstairs to investigate the source of my piercing, heart-wrenching sobs and asked what had happened. I was crumpled on the floor, tearing my wet, soapy hands through my hair in endless agony.

All I could do was cry. I cried those deep, wracking sobs that had escaped only a few times before when the limit of my capacity had been reached but this time, I had endless capacity for the agony because I had purposefully spent the last few years making room for it.

I cried until I physically couldn't cry anymore and then, after resting and recuperating, my body gave up on energy conservation and cried again. It went on like this for hours until I decided to call Rachel and asked her if she had any immediate openings. Miraculously, she did and as Brandon drove me to her office, still not knowing all the details, she immediately knew that a major shift had occurred.

She helped me take one of the TheraTapper pulsers for EMDR in each hand and turned it on before guiding me into my Sanctuary. The combination of my mental safe space and the vibrations of the pulsers helped me ground down enough to catch my breath and explain what had happened. I told her everything. I told her about the details of what I had done to my brother when I was six and he was four. I told her that I, myself, had experienced sexual abuse as a child (something I had kept from her until then). And I told her that it had been my Oma, my mom's mom, who did it.

Even as I write this I still feel an echo of the excruciating pain I felt when I first said that out loud.

I loved my Oma. She was a little, old German woman who was incredibly funny, made delicious apple pancakes, and had an imaginary butler named Henry who she'd boss around the house, making him do her dishes and cook us breakfast before quietly cleaning the plates as I watched *Pocahontas*. But she was also the person who threw temper tantrums when she took me to Olive Garden that were sometimes so obscene that I, as a grade school child, would apologize to the manager and help her calm down on the way out to the car because I couldn't offer to drive her myself and I needed her to be sane enough to drive us home. She was the woman who told my parents she could, "only handle one of them at a time," in reference to our sleepovers. My siblings and I could all sleep over at my other grandma Judy's house on the same night where we'd wake up on the big pull-out couch and watch *Looney*

Toons and eat Pop-Tarts the next morning but we never, *never ever* slept over at Oma's house together. She said she preferred to keep us separate. And now I know why. She always said I should sleep in the bed next to her because her bed was the best—even when I begged to sleep on the couch. She gave me baths when I didn't want them, even when I tried to be smart and convince my mom to give me a bath right before going over to her house in the first place. But my mom's baths were never good enough, she'd say, she had to give me a special bath herself. And as I lay in her bed at night I cried, even though I didn't know why and I asked God why the warm glass of milk she gave me tasted funny and why my limbs were heavy. I asked him why I couldn't move and why the ghouls were watching me from the doorway and I asked him why she had to snore so loud because I couldn't sleep with her making noise and I asked him why every bone and muscle and fiber in my body was screaming.

These memories tore my heart apart.

Rachel helped guide me into a relatively manageable mental space. Brandon had been waiting for me in the lounge. I got in the car and we drove home in a silence only pockmarked by my hiccups.

Then, somehow, I continued to live.

It was hard.

"Hard" is an understatement but that's the word I've always used. It was hard to try and do regular life shit after that. For the first two months, I was barely able to function. Thankfully, by that point, I had an at-home job that I could easily work around my random crying fits. GoKart had been acquired right before the pandemic hit and my position was cut. I had tried a few other jobs but finally was offered a position with a major insurance company and joined the team that was restating all of their plans and documents. It was a big project and as long as I got my work done and showed up on a call once a week I was in the clear with no micromanagement. I took a lot of breaks to go cry during those months. It was exactly the job I needed to get through that time.

Helping me every day in ways I can't even begin to fully recount were Brandon and our newly adopted dog, a pittie mix we named Daruk after the Goron champion in a new Legend of Zelda game called *Breath of the Wild*. He was 85 pounds of snuggly love whose favorite toys were basketballs and anything you could throw, but Daruk had also experienced some shit and could go from happy-go-lucky pooch to a shaking, terrified ball of fur at the slightest sharp sound. Just like Roody-Roo all those years before, Daruk knew that I wasn't ok and started helping me soften my heart again day after day, week after week, month after month. We helped to heal each other as Brandon helped to heal us both.

Brandon became not only the most empathetic man I had ever known, but the most loving one as well. Knowing all of the pieces, I had sunk into a depression of deep self-hatred once again. I felt disgusting. I felt unclean. I felt like I *almost* wanted to die again but I reminded myself over and over that I had already chosen to live **no matter what**. I told Brandon I wouldn't hold it against him if he wanted to break up with me because now he knew what I knew—but he stayed and told me he saw someone so beautiful on both the inside and the outside that he couldn't *not* love them. I withdrew into myself, falling into the endless guilt and apologizing for not going out or socially engaging—Brandon said there was nothing to apologize for and asked if I was ok with a hug, seeking permission for physical touch to support my temporary boundaries before holding me close as I cried into his chest. Even when we didn't have sex for six months and then infrequently for a whole year after that he still said he wanted me in his life. He showed up for me in ways I never imagined a human being could.

Eventually, slowly but surely, my boys helped me get back on the healing pathway I had started. I settled into my new normal, picked up my nightmares again, and tried to find a way to live with the full truth of *everything*.

10
The "F" Word

The art of healing oneself begins with observation and acknowledgment. As we begin to observe and acknowledge how we truly feel, what we actually think, and who we really want to be, things will naturally begin to progress toward a healing experience. We see our memories, feel what needs to be felt, and move through the stages of grief for what we could have been or what we could have experienced. Along that unique healing pathway, we find a truth at the heart of our journey: that we are the ones causing our own *continued* pain and suffering.

This is the most empowering concept I can teach you. It means that you truly *do* have all the power necessary to heal yourself.

But this truth was also the most difficult for me to learn and I needed to experience it in my own way to comprehend it. So if the following words are dissonant or grating for you, that's ok. All I ask is that you remain open to the idea of it so that perhaps someday you may come to understand and experience it in your own way.

There are many different people in my life who have hurt me and there are many moments where I endured suffering at the hands of another. I *was* a victim in the moments that those individuals used or abused me. But through my healing experience, I realized that I am *not* a victim of those moments anymore.

Today I am only a victim of myself. I am a victim of the narratives and beliefs that I chose to take on in order to survive. I am a victim of the narratives that *I* chose to uphold. Stick with me here, I promise this is going somewhere even if you're thinking, *Meg, you were a child, you didn't choose this.* I know, and I agree, but stick with me.

When I suffered sexually abusive acts and then reenacted those abuses upon my brother I took on the beliefs that I was a bad person, that I was guilty, and that I was worthless. When my parents physically beat me or tortured me and then told me that I was overreacting and that I couldn't tell anyone else about it I took on the narratives that I was just weak and that *I* was the one who was shameful. Those beliefs were necessary at the time, helping me to stay small and meet the expectations of my family system and childhood environment because I couldn't leave them, and it wasn't yet safe for me to explore my traumas. If I had opened the box then, I may not have written this book today. But over the years, even after it was safe to explore the box, I continued to hold onto those beliefs, refusing to change my internal narrative out of perceived necessity because I was too afraid to love myself.

I was too afraid to love myself.

How could I love the little girl who had abused her best friend, her brother? How could I love the adult woman I had become who had cut out her own parents from her life? How could I love someone who had wanted to kill themself?

I was too afraid to love myself.

I was too afraid to love the teenager who watched her siblings being beaten and didn't call CPS. I was too afraid to love the kid who was manipulated and then manipulated others in turn. I was too afraid to love the child who had walked into the woods and tried to hang herself. I was too afraid of loving a little girl who had been tortured by a grandparent.

I didn't think she was worthy of love.

But the more time I spent with that little girl, the child, the teenager, observing and acknowledging her memories and feelings, the more I allowed myself to feel her pain and understand her suffering and I realized what a resilient, powerful, loving being she had been *the whole time.*

She wasn't a bad person, she was a hurt person, and sometimes hurt people hurt other people as an expression of the original pain they experienced but she wasn't hurting people now. She wasn't guilty, she felt responsible for her actions because she loved her brother and wanted to make things right. And she wasn't worthless, she was worthy of everything this world had to offer simply because she existed and *tried* to love others.

It's ok that she was hurt. It's ok that she had wanted to die. It's ok that she estranged the people who raised her. She had to find her own way through the shit and she did. She had never really stopped loving herself.

She, *I*, moved through my fears and memories one by one until I learned that I have *always* loved that little girl.

I have always loved myself.

I can't pinpoint the exact moment it happened but when I finally, *fully* found love for myself I realized that *this* is what forgiveness truly is. The "F" word.

Forgiveness was a concept I used to despise. I avoided using it like many parents of young children try to avoid using the actual "F" word—say it with me now, "FUCK!" (Remember, verbal swearing can relieve stress). My Catholic upbringing and family system mutilated my relationship with the concept of forgiveness through years of programming me to be a sinner. I was falsely taught that forgiveness was "taking the high road" which I interpreted as just choosing to be better than others, or that forgiveness was "letting go of your anger for someone else's actions" which I interpreted as letting someone get away with sinning because God would give them their due later, and when I got in a fight with my siblings our parents would say, "just be the bigger person and forgive them and move on" which indicated to me that my problems weren't worth the time it took to figure them out and I should just let people do whatever they pleased because our family image mattered the most.

Today, I can tell you for a certainty, that is NOT what forgiveness is.

Forgiveness is allowing yourself to love regardless of what you have done or what has been done unto you.

Love is a complicated emotion.

Love is Grief. Love is Joy. Love is Anger. Love is Peace. Love is Sorrow. Love can be beautiful and horrible and expansive and soul-sucking all at the same time. Love cannot be put in a box (though we sometimes try) and love is everywhere on the planet and in every human being in one form or another. Love is Love.

Love comes in different shapes and sizes and capacities. Some people have small love. Some people have a literal metric ton of love. But love can be found everywhere.

If forgiveness is allowing yourself to love regardless of what you have done or what has been done unto you, and if love can be found everywhere in a multitude of forms, then forgiveness can be found everywhere too, in every person and in every situation.

I found love for the little girl that was me, the girl that had wanted to die. I forgave her and held her and loved her as I put the pieces of myself back together again. And as I discovered my love for her, I discovered that I still loved my parents even though they had hurt me in so many ways and even though I will forever maintain our estrangement. I love them because all those moments that were good, all those moments where we laughed and ate ice cream and went on camping trips and danced to silly songs and thought Enya was singing "BUR-PING SEA-GULLS" instead of Cursum Perficio (seriously, google that shit, it's hilarious), still exist in my memory. The good memories are a part of my total experience. The love still exists.

The loving memories don't outweigh the fucked up shit though—the times I was threatened or beaten or felt fingers and green beans and bile in my throat all at the same time—because *there is no comparison.* There is no *only* good or *only* bad. There is a spectrum of experiences.

In some moments my parents showed me true love and in others they showed me their own suffering and enacted their pain upon me but love still existed. I love my parents even though I see the rest of my life without them. I forgave my parents and in forgiving them I didn't "let them off the hook" or "took the high road" I chose to honor my own capacity for the love that still exists in my heart. I chose to love the memories of love. I love them and am still angry with them all at the same time because I recognize that *I am the totality of my experiences.* And that can be forgiveness.

I love my Oma too. I hated her for a long while, yes, but hate is another form of love. I hated her because I should have been able to *wholly* love her. I should have been able to trust her and count on her to protect me and love me in the ways that grandmas are supposed to love their grandchildren. I hated her because she caused me pain and suffering and harm. But I also loved her, and I have chosen to still feel that love. I love her for all the times that she took us to the Mines of Spain on beautiful walks in the woods. I love her for all the funny faces she'd make. I love her for all the wild stories she'd share about swimming up the Rhine in Germany to steal lemons and apples when she was a kid during WWII—she and her cousins would stuff the fruit into their bathing suits and pretend they were funny boobs before swimming away. She always made those stories humorous even though I knew they were dark because she was starving. I love her because those loving, funny memories still exist even though they sit right next to the ones that hated her.

Here on planet Earth we experience time linearly but we are time travelers whenever we place ourselves in past memories or think forward into what we may experience in the future. We carry with us into every moment the totality of our experiences. I have loved and loathed the same people all within this single lifetime and forgiveness is allowing myself to feel all those things in their totality while still choosing to love.

It's ok to still love the people who have hurt you as long as you love and respect yourself above all.

For me, that looks like maintaining estrangement from my parents for the foreseeable future. I respect myself and know that they are not safe people for me but I still allow myself to share the loving, funny stories I remember and laugh about them too. I love myself and want to protect my peace. Healthy boundaries are what help me show up in the world the way that I want to and share the love I have discovered with the people who love me in healthy ways.

It's ok to love with the fullness of my being because that's what forgiveness is: allowing yourself to love and remember love, despite everything that you have ever done or experienced.

Forgiveness is allowing yourself to know and feel and be everything that *you* need to be. It's complicated. There's no step-by-step process to get there and it can mean different things to different people but to me, forgiveness is allowing myself to love.

I don't remember exactly when I began exploring the love in my memories again—it was a gradual process, sometimes time *is* the healer—but eventually it was just there. Love was there when I realized that the only thing I am responsible for is living my own life with love. Love was there when I realized that I wanted to protect my peace and that it really was ok for me to estrange myself from my parents to uphold that. Love was there when I realized that by protecting my peace and living life lovingly, I was directly impacting the lives around me for the better.

I could have chosen to stew in my misery, reliving the horrible memories every day for the rest of my life, remaining entrenched in the nightmare but instead I saw that *I had a choice.*

I chose to heal and move on and live.

I dove back into my work with Rachel and continued processing those memories that had lain dormant for so many years. It was hard—it fucking sucked—but I did it anyway. I pushed myself beyond anything I thought I was capable of because I wanted to live a life full of love. I wanted to find joy again. I wanted to explore a lifetime of love with Brandon. I wanted to share my kindness with the world. I wanted to love more than I wanted to suffer.

So I tried.

I worked through all of the emotions I had ever felt. A common misconception is that when you work "through" your emotions you're clearing them out. I've found that to be false. When I worked through my emotions I held them all and made room in my heart for each and every one of them for the rest of eternity. I opened my capacity to the fullness of my experience. I screamed and cried and punched pillows and cursed more than I ever had in the Marine Corps (which is saying something) and made room for those emotions to stay with me because they're a part of me. I never expelled them, I let them be what they needed to be and then held their memory.

Every emotion is valid and by working through my emotions I popped the top off the bottle and let the pressure release in a healthy way. Today, I have anger and grief and love and joy in my heart all at the same time but they're on an even playing field now. I'm no longer consumed by guilt but sometimes I still feel guilty. I no longer hate myself but sometimes I still feel unworthy. I no longer get entrenched in several hour-long, cycling panic attacks a day but I still feel panicky sometimes. And that's ok. Healing is a life-long process.

Now, I let myself feel whatever emotions come up, ask where they came from or what triggered them, and then address their root right on the spot, maintaining a relative sense of balance.

As I felt through all of my emotions and began to explore self-love and the old "F" word (forgiveness), I felt ready to call my brother in April of 2021.

We hadn't talked much over the years but we texted every once in a while and checked in with each other so it wasn't completely out of the blue. I prefaced our call with a note that said I wanted to talk about some difficult things and that I wanted him to make sure he was in a safe space throughout our conversation just in case.

When he answered the phone my words shook as soon as they began falling out of my mouth but I persevered and continued onward. I told him everything that I remembered about abusing him and being abused myself, I told him about the psychological and physical abuse I was processing from our parents, and I told him about how I had chosen to live a new life. I apologized to him, acknowledging that even though I had been a child I knew I had still hurt him and I was so, so, so very sorry. I said I didn't know if he remembered any of this and I was sorry if he didn't until now and that I was going to be there for him in any way that he needed, even if he never wanted to speak to me again. I had worked myself up, dreading his response, but finally quieted down to let him speak. He was silent for a while before drawing in a breath.

"Megan," he said. "I've known the whole time and I've never held it against you."

I burst into tears. Never, *never*, in a million years had I expected his first words to be so truly forgiving. I was overcome with awe and love and respect. A part of me felt like I didn't deserve it but a larger part of me allowed myself to receive the love that was offered. I recovered through my tears and we chatted a bit longer before calling it a day, ending our conversation with a sense of peace, understanding, and a love that I now knew was possible.

11
Progressions

When you step onto your unique healing pathway you'll find moments of pause where you look back and see how far you've come. It's important to acknowledge these moments as points of tangible progress. They help you find the strength to keep doing the healing work even when you might feel crippled by grief. As I regained my memories, picked myself up, allowed myself to love, and found a new way to live with the totality of my experiences I leaned on my markers of tangible progress.

There were physical and psychological changes that manifested in the waking world but I had been so high-functioning for so long that many people in my life simply didn't notice—but Brandon and I did. My panic attacks began to decrease in both frequency and intensity, I found myself laughing more (even after knowing everything!), and I found joy in life again. But the easiest way to observe my own progress was through the nightmares that had begun turning into dreams: my progressions.

A progression dream or nightmare is a series that often starts out as recurring but changes and resolves itself over time. Recurring dreams are just as their name implies: recurrent. There's no set limit or quantifiable number to define a recurring dream but they often have similar content, emotions, locations, or themes among them—they do not have to be exactly the same every time to be classified as part of the same series. I have had many recurring dreams and nightmares throughout my life and many of those have turned into resolutive dreams, especially during this last part of my healing experience.

Before stepping onto my healing pathway, I used to have a recurring nightmare that took place in the closet with my brother in our childhood home. My mom would walk in, see us, and then turn into a terrifying creature that was half demon, half ghost-like being from Edvard Munch's painting *The Scream*. The nightmare would place a black cloak of endless guilt upon me as my mom would scream and scream and scream about how awful of a person I was. I'd wake in a sweat, completely shaken.

This nightmare is pretty self-explanatory: I was reliving my memories and the emotions that had gotten stuck there. But over time, as I allowed myself to sit with the guilt and worthlessness, exploring why they had rooted there, the nightmare began to change. Sometimes I'd get up and start to walk away from the closet before my mom even entered the room. In other versions of the nightmare my mom would soften. Her screams would turn to yells which would then become a stern but even tone. Eventually, the dreams moved out of the closet all together, removed my brother from the scenario and homed in on the narrative with my mom—her imagery represented the root of my limiting beliefs. I began standing up for myself and arguing with her in the nightmare, asking why she wasn't helping me or why she thought I was a piece of shit.

Today, I know that these nightmares were a psychological reflection of the emotional work I was doing to clear up my internal narrative. Parts work, or Internal Family Systems (IFS), is a concept that Rachel introduced me to and it was incredibly helpful for me to explore during my healing experience. The basic theory is that we're an amalgamation of different parts and some of our parts are thrown out of whack through life's experiences, becoming dissonant and actively creating conflict in our own lives in an attempt to be helpful. Our dissonant parts start to act out and IFS, psychological therapy, and healing work in general can help those dissonant parts find a new way to coexist with the rest of ourselves for a fully-functioning system once again.

I believe that we enter this world as whole beings and that all of the parts of our soul and personality easily work together. Then life happens and we're exposed to challenges and difficulties and sometimes other people's shit. When we're exposed to these things and don't yet have the tools to work through them, some of our parts sacrifice themselves by moving out of alignment and taking over the driver's seat to get us through the moment. It's a survival mechanism.

As an example, I often worked with Rachel on my guilty part whom I named Truthsayer. Whenever I imagined Truthsayer in my mind's eye I saw my mom from that recurring nightmare in the closet and she was screaming at me, berating me and telling me I was worthless. This part of myself believed, in truth, that I was guilty. Over time, I realized that Truthsayer wasn't a part of myself that I needed to get rid of, Truthsayer *originally* used to lift me up and help me explore the truth of the universe. When my mom was screaming at me for hurting my brother I didn't know how to handle it or what to do in that moment so the part of me that was connected to my universal truth bravely stepped in and donned the cloak of guilt. Guilt actually kept me alive for some time. Guilt kept me small and convinced me not to interact with my brother anymore out of fear which soothed my mom and prevented any further outbursts along that line of thought. But Truthsayer, the guilty part that endured, kept piling on the guilt long after I could have had the tools to meet her and help her come back into balance. She began actively detracting from my life because she was hurting. Truthsayer was the part of me that created my panic attacks, prevented me from engaging in situations that could potentially be verbally hurtful, and kept me small to avoid being seen and, potentially, screamed at.

As I worked with my Truthsayer part, I held her and acknowledged that while she had helped me at one point in time, we were changing and it was safe to step back into her original function once again. It took a lot of convincing but after a while, as I pointed out to myself over and over again that no one was screaming at me now, she began to return to balance—*I* began to return to balance. My recurring nightmare with Truthsayer, represented by my mom's image in the dreamspace, shifted the more I dreamed. Eventually, we would end up just talking in the nightmare and it wasn't so terrifying. Sometimes she even quietly apologized for hurting me.

One day, the nightmare formally became a dream. In the dream, I found myself not in the room with the closet but in the foyer looking at a bunch of boxes sitting in a pile in the living room. My mom was nowhere to be found so I started walking through my childhood home room-by-room. I encountered memories in this place but they weren't horrifying anymore, just simple reflections, like an echo. Each room held its own tiny story. Finally, I found my mom (Truthsayer) packing up the kitchen cupboards and asked her what she was doing. She said she was moving on. She was grateful for this home but it didn't feel right to her anymore. She was ready to sell it and excited to see what was waiting for her on the other side.

I never had another nightmare in that childhood house again and almost every time I've encountered my mom in the dream space since, she's been my friend or she's been there to help me, though we haven't spoken in years in waking life. The mom part of my internal narrative has become the truest Truthsayer.

This is a progression, a series of recurring nightmares that found resolution and turned into a dream over time.

I've experienced other progressions as well, most of them being located in homes or buildings familiar to my childhood. After Revelation Day my subconscious revisited that earlier nightmare in my Oma's basement. They were horrible nightmares at first and, quite obviously, explored horrible memories but over time even those nightmares softened and shifted. Eventually, I'd approach the little girl in the basement, lift her up into my arms, and carry her upstairs where we'd sit on Oma's back porch and admire the ladybugs. That progression ended with us, myself as a little girl and I as an adult, walking across the road to the Mines of Spain for a hike that filled me with the joy of life instead of the need to leave it. I never found my nightmares located in that basement again.

Progress can be measured in a multitude of ways. We can observe the lessening of our physical symptoms, the progressions in our dreamspace, and noticeable changes in the ways we think.

The more I worked through my pain, the more I felt everything I ever had needed to feel, the more capacity I had for love and the more the universe filled that new, beautifully expansive space in my heart with joy.

12
Resolution

I felt like I was being pulled from behind. Brushing the feeling off, I continued exploring my dream but the tugging continued. Suddenly, I snapped into my bedroom, conscious and alert but completely unable to move. A feeling of immense terror, the most I had ever felt, wrapped itself around me, but instead of succumbing to its weight I felt a spark of anger ignite within my core.

I was done with this shit.

I fought against the heaviness of sleep paralysis with every ounce of willpower I had and turned my head to the left. There, standing in front of my closet door was the woman cloaked in black with an intricate lace veil over her face. I had seen her more times than I could count in my nightmares but this time I *truly* saw her. She turned to look at me and I felt the fullness of recognition deep within my soul. *She was me.* She was the part of me that felt totally consumed by fear. As she moved towards my bed and grabbed my left ankle she actually succeeded in pulling me onto the floor for the first time.

I ignited.

The power of my anger grew into a magnificent force. This was a contest of wills and I tapped into every ounce of strength and resilience in my being to help me through this. I felt the light of knowledge and the power of self-loving forgiveness surge through my limbs. Shaking off the last remnants of paralysis into a state of lucidity, I dug deep and *willed* myself to stand up, rising to my feet until I finally stood on solid ground in my recurring sleep paralysis nightmare.

The woman backed up in surprise, realizing that her fear was no longer keeping me restrained. I began to walk towards her, slowly planting one foot in front of the other. As I walked, the pointer finger of my right hand began to glow. I came face to face with the woman and strongly poked her in the chest saying, "If you are not of the light, leave now."

My fingertip grew brighter and I poked her again, "If you are not of the light, *leave now!*"

A hole began to form in her chest as if she were made of paper and someone had started a blaze in the middle, consuming her from the inside out.

I poked her a third time, screaming with all the power in my soul, "If you are not of *my* light, you MUST. LEAVE. NOW!"

The light at the end of my finger exploded with radiance, shining into every crevice of my room and blasting the woman into a million pieces.

I woke up, this time for real, and felt the fear washing away.

I had my last fear-based sleep paralysis nightmare on December 20th, 2021.

For a while I thought the veiled woman might come back in another capacity or that another sleep paralysis nightmare would take her place, but I had truly healed that part of me and never saw her again. It's been almost three whole years now as I write this.

Today, I have the occasional psychological nightmare but they're nothing compared to the weight of terror I used to experience. When I wake up from a nightmare now I turn on the light and simply record it (usually typing it to myself in the note app on my phone). I identify the fear that was present in the dream and ask myself where I feel that same fear in my life right now. Once I comprehend it, I look at that area of my life and ask how I can change it for the better. I take action on each and every nightmare, using them as helpful tools instead of being consumed by their fear. I understand now that they've been here to help me all along.

I have found the brilliance and joy of dreams again. Sometimes they're fantastical, sometimes they're psychological, but in either case I always find useful information within them about myself. At the end of the day, our dreams are the observations of our own internal conversations, and I begin each day by recording what I can remember, observing myself, and asking where I can apply my own wisdom.

Healing is an ever-evolving process and there's never one check-in-the-box that says you've fully healed. I still experience symptoms of my childhood C-PTSD but I manage the triggers well and they rarely affect my life in truly negative ways anymore. I still experience symptoms of my military-related PTSD, avoiding fireworks shows and going home early from our family cookout on the Fourth of July. But it's ok, I know my limits and I take care of myself through them. I still experience panic attacks from time to time but instead of cycling through their intensity for a couple of hours, I resolve them in less than ten minutes.

For me, this is what being healed looks like.

I can never unknow everything that I know just as I can never unsee what I have seen but I have found a loving way to live with it. I have acknowledged every part of my life, I have felt through everything I needed to feel, and I have released myself from the societal and familial narratives that once kept me locked in a cycle of pain. I say that I am healed because I've not only found what works for me, I've found a life full of peace and love and fulfillment *as a result* of everything I have ever experienced.

I was my own greatest catalyst for change and I am my own magnificent healer. *You* have that same power and by acknowledging your life's experiences you can heal your nightmares too—the ones you experience in dreamtime and the ones you've lived through.

To heal your nightmares, you first need to *want* to heal. Make the choice to try, step onto your unique healing pathway, and enter your right time. Next, spend some time curating your right place. Take a look at the totality of your environment, acknowledge the people, places, and elements of your day-to-day existence and make some adjustments by letting go of the elements that do not support you and seeking out new elements that do. After entering your right place, align yourself with a psychological, emotional, or spiritual guide—someone to provide you with the knowledge and space necessary to move through your frozen roots. Show up for yourself, try the techniques and mechanisms presented to you, and begin building your toolbox. Pay attention to your nightmares, write them down, and hold them. Ask them to show you what you need to know and then observe their wisdom. Allow time to play its part and keep on going. Your life *will* change for the better and you'll discover your own unique definition for living a healed and loving existence.

This has been a book about nightmares and how to use their wisdom to heal your life. *You* are your own greatest catalyst for change. *You* are the healer you've been waiting for.

Afterword

Writing this book has been life changing. When I first set out to begin filling the pages it was intended to be a self-help book with a collection of nightmare interpretation examples from my podcast *The Dream Axis* but something about that didn't feel quite right. A few brief iterations passed and I put it on the forever backburner... until I woke up from a dream one morning and knew exactly what it needed to be: my memoir.

I thought I had processed all there ever was to process but in writing this book I have healed even more. The ability to observe my life from a linear perspective has been beautiful. In my head, everything was just kind of mashed together until I began the writing process and worked on extricating each individual piece. Now, here on the other side, I have a much greater appreciation for the choices I made, the gravity of what I came through, and have given myself even more grace than I originally thought possible which has carried over into my life today.

Brandon and I got married in the fall of 2021 and have continued building and living our life together. We're surrounded by the most amazing friends and family I could have ever asked for. Ironically, we recently moved back to the same Minneapolis neighborhood where we met at a board game night all those years ago and it's a sweet, loving anecdote in our ongoing story. Every day heals me more.

Through writing this book, the most recent act of healing I've experienced was opening myself to the idea of being a mother. Within the first few months of dating Brandon, I told him that I liked where our relationship was going but he needed to know that I didn't want to have children. I like kids but I knew I didn't have the capacity for them while in the middle of my journey and, unbeknownst to me until recently, I had embodied a limiting narrative that I *shouldn't* have kids because of everything that I had ever experienced. I was terrified of turning into those who had hurt me and vowed never to pass that pain on. For his part, Brandon had seen himself as a father but wanted to be with me more so he said that was just fine and we continued on living, checking in with each other on the kid front every six months or so to ensure we were still aligned.

About a week after I finished writing the first draft of this book, the limiting narrative that I shouldn't have kids simply snapped off. I was reading at an art festival that Saturday (sometimes I have a booth at fairs in the Twin Cities) when a little three-year-old boy came up to me at 10:30 in the morning and pointed excitedly at the stars on my table cover. He promptly plopped himself down on the pavement and sang the entirety of *Twinkle Twinkle Little Star*. It was beyond captivating and adorable! For the rest of the day children just kept coming up to me. I talked to kids who had seen Sasquatch in their dreams, some of them liked the cool rocks on my table, and others just wanted to ask me random questions like, "Why is your hair so curly?!" or "Do you dream about fairies too?"

Fifteen minutes before closing, a grandma pushing her one-year-old grandchild in a stroller ran up to my table and asked if I still had time for a quick reading and we sat down to chat. Her granddaughter was quiet but kept smiling at me the whole time. When we finished, the grandma found herself falling into a spiraling line of personal questions again, something we had talked about in the reading, until the baby broke our line of conversation and declared that we were, "All done!"

"All done!" she cried happily. "All done! All done!"

We laughed and, suddenly, I felt that limiting narrative lift off.

Baby fever hit me full force. I sucked in my breath and didn't know what to think. The grandma and I went our separate ways, Brandon helped me pack up my booth, and we went home. But that realization continued to reverberate through my being like the brightest star. It grew and grew and grew until I knew, without a doubt, that I not only wanted to be a mother, but that I would be a damn good one too.

I brought it up to Brandon and through our conversation I realized that it had been easier for me to lie to myself about wanting to have kids than admit that I believed I shouldn't have them because of my own trauma. I had been denying myself something that I truly wanted out of deep fear and had finally surfaced above it. Brandon jumped on board way more quickly than I thought he would, excited to once again explore a dream he had let go of when he met me.

I'm not sure if we'll ever actually have kids but the fact that I now understand myself so fully that it's an option once again is absolutely bonkers. I have healed SO. VERY. MUCH. And I want you to know, dear reader, that even after you think you've healed everything, life just keeps on healing.

Thank you so much for reading this book. As an independent author, it would mean the world to me if you rated or reviewed this book online. Every comment, every share, and every mention of this book helps to spread its message of love and hope across the landscape of time. In this, I graciously ask for your assistance.

May the universe place unending blessings upon you and may healing be an ever-present experience in your life.

With love,
Meg Renfri Bartlett

Exploration and Interpretation

A Brief Note on Interpretation

There are over 8 billion different ways to interpret dreams and nightmares at the time of this writing—as many ways as there are people on the planet. This is because each individual person works with their own unique symbolic language. A dreamer's symbolic language is a reflection of their life in totality. It takes into account their distinctive life experiences, the emotions they felt during and after those experiences, the thoughts and narratives they developed as a result, and their original soul signature or nature of being. No human on this earth can exactly replicate another's life in totality, therefore, each individual has their own unique symbolic language.

To put this into context, let's examine the dream imagery of a dog. If you google "meaning of dog in dream" or something similar you'll get a myriad of different answers and suggestions about partnerships, loyalty, trust, etc. These are common definitions that can be true for some people, but they don't take into account an individual's totality, which is what matters most.

Personally, I love dogs but I also have a complicated relationship with them (as you may have already read about in this book). When I dream about a dog, he usually represents something that I feel deeply responsible for or sometimes even the exploration of personal worth, not the concept of loyalty or trust. And if a person who had been viciously attacked by a dog at some point in their life dreamed of one, it would clearly have a different meaning to them also—something fear-based or a representation of perceived danger depending on their stage of resolution and healing from the original experience. These are two very different definitions for the same piece of symbolic imagery and differ from the "common" definition found in dream dictionary resources, clearly indicating that an individual's totality is the true identifier of symbolic language.

This is why you will always be your own best dream and nightmare interpreter.

Online dream resources and dream dictionaries are not completely useless though, in fact, I have one that I bought when I was sixteen that I still use from time to time when I come across something new in the dream space. These resources are most helpful as a starting point for ideas on what a piece of imagery *could* mean for you, as long as you follow up with your own context when using one. And sometimes these resources *can* be spot on in their definitions because we, as human beings, have many similar experiences.

As far as full dream and nightmare interpretations go, my advice is not to get hung up on the details when you're beginning to learn your unique symbolic language. Take your best guess and use your emotions or the feelings within the dream or nightmare as a guide.

The emotions that you experience during the dream or nightmare *and* after waking are always the key! Ask yourself where in your waking life you are feeling (or have felt in the past) those same emotions. Follow that thread and let your gut tell you the rest.

When I write out detailed interpretations of my own dreams and nightmares I begin by making a list of the key elements. I don't have to list everything in the dream but I try to identify the most prominent pieces to me. After I create my list, I briefly define those individual elements and list out the emotions. Once I have all that information, I weave it together into an interpretation which is just a collection of sentences that give meaning to my experience. It doesn't have to be like writing a novel nor does it need to be completely structured.

The following section details my interpretations of the nightmares in this book. Hopefully, they give you a good idea of how to get started interpreting your own dreams and nightmares. There are many excellent dream books out there but not many on nightmares so you'll also find a list of common nightmares, their definitions, and the questions to ask when you experience them in the next section (*A Compendium of Common Nightmares*).

Remember, you are always your own best dream and nightmare interpreter and it's important to take your totality into context. For each main element, ask yourself if you've ever had an experience with that element or image before and trust the first thoughts that come up. Interpretations are an excellent way to get to know yourself and dive into the story of *you*.

Creature-in-the-Depths Nightmare

Elements

1. Sea/Body of Water: In almost every culture across the planet water represents the concept of emotion. We are 70% water, when we feel strong emotions our eyes leak water, and we are born through water.

2. Monster Shadow: Something I know is there and something I fear but can't quite "see" or understand. Its true form is still hidden.

3. Ship: A vessel keeping me afloat. Refuge.

4. Tidal Wave: An emotion that's threatening to drown or consume me. Something massive and unavoidable.

5. Leviathan: For me, the king of monsters, the thing I fear most.

6. (The Monster's) Eyes: We have many phrases about eyes such as, "eyes are the windows to the soul," and they can represent sight, seeing, knowing and truth.

Emotions

Fear, terror, dread, panic, abandoned/alone

Interpretation

The storminess of the waters in this nightmare reflects the stormy emotions I found myself mired in, setting the scene for an exploration of my emotional state. As I look over the side of the deck and see the monster's shadow, I know that there's something I fear to see within the depths of my emotion and memory, but I can't quite make it out. The shadow represents the memories that I have purposely avoided but I can no longer ignore their presence even if I don't yet understand them.

My ship, the thing that has been holding me above the surface of my emotions, is damaged by the storm. It can't take much more of a beating—I can't handle much more avoidance, my emotions are wearing me down. Sooner or later, I'm going to have to swim (or sink). In a moment of clarity, I run to get help (alert the captain) but realize I'm the only one here. I feel completely alone facing this memory that I fear.

A tidal wave looms over me, representing the inevitable crash of emotion that contains the memory (represented by the leviathan). Furthermore, when I think of the snake-like body of the leviathan I remember the bible story of the Garden of Eden and the snake that told Eve to eat the fruit of the Tree of Knowledge. There's an old sense of danger here with religious undertones, I'm terrified of knowing what the leviathan (the memory) is. The snake-like imagery also represents my family's narrative of avoidance—that we shouldn't dig things up that could be difficult, that we should avoid pain, that the knowledge is forbidden because it could destroy the false sense of security I have surrounded myself with.

Finally, the leviathan's eyes represent the truth of knowledge and the identity of that memory. Even the yellow of the eyes can be helpful: I associate the color yellow with the solar plexus chakra which is related to our center of personal power and self-worth. This memory (the leviathan) holds the truth preventing me from connecting to my natural sense of personal power.

Application

At the time I was experiencing this recurring nightmare, I recognized it was telling me that something was wrong and that I was overwhelmed with the emotion of fear, but I didn't understand much else. Regardless, this nightmare convinced me to seek out psychological therapy in Seattle, something I truly needed and benefitted from. My nightmare still helped me even though I didn't fully comprehend its meaning at the time.

If someone were to come to me today with this nightmare I would give them my interpretation, check to make sure that it resonates with them (adjusting definitions as needed based on their unique totality and symbolic language), and then suggest that they seek assistance diving into their fear-based memories. I would suggest that they explore where their personal sense of power feels like it's been taken away.

I would ask them the following questions for self-reflection:

- What are you afraid of knowing?

- What have you been avoiding?

- Why do you feel like you need to stay on the surface of your emotions?

The Cat and the Ghouls

Most dreams and nightmares can be interpreted through the psychological lens because the bulk of our experiences here on earth exist in present, conscious, very psychological moments but some dreams and nightmares are beyond psychological comprehension. This nightmare was more than a psychological dream, crossing into the territory of the spiritual and what exists beyond the human experience.

First, this dream felt like a 10/10 on my *gravity scale*. The gravity scale is a tool I've created for identifying spiritually significant dreams and can be applied to nightmares as well. Basically, it's the WHOA factor of a dream or nightmare as rated on a scale from 1-10 where 1 = a purely "meh" psychological dream (like looking for a toilet or doing laundry) and 10 = a super profound sense of WHOA (like receiving a visitation from a loved one who's passed away or meeting an extraterrestrial being). The level 1 dreams still have important information (bathroom dreams usually indicate that we need to let go of what no longer serves us and doing laundry in the dream space usually indicates a need to clean up our attitude or give ourselves a refresh in waking life), but the 10/10 dreams are particularly important to note and the more you record them, the more you can identify similarities among them which can help you understand more about your personal spiritual context. I recommend rating each dream in your dream journal (or recording app—I just text my dreams to myself at this point) so you can go back and review all of your 10/10s for possible similarities.

Back to my cat and the ghouls nightmare, I personally believe this one was somewhat "real." Now reality can mean many different things to many different people and it's ok if you don't agree with me, but I really do believe that some darker entities stopped by when I was a kid because there was a lot of dark shit that happened in that childhood home and like attracts like. However, there's no need to be afraid because they really can't hurt you—it's a law of the universe. Only other humans can affect humans and that takes place in waking life. Anything that's of a darker vibration that visits you is there either because there's something within *yourself* that it resonates with or because you created it in the first place (which we'll get to with sleep paralysis demons in the following interpretations). When we encounter dark things in the dreamspace it's a call to do some self-exploration and identify what within you or around you is sending out that signal so that you can resolve it and send any beings on their way.

As far as the cat goes, I truly believe that she was an astral messenger. The astral realm is a theoretical plane of existence beyond the physical where non-human energies can exist. There are many ways to explain it across cultures and religions, but I see the astral plane as just another layer that overlaps here on earth. I believe there are things around me that exist but that I cannot see because they don't have physical bodies, they have energetic ones and my eyes have forgotten how to see them when I stepped into this existence.

However, in the dreamspace (or nightmarespace) these astral beings communicate and interact with us using visual imagery and sense of knowing. In the dream space, we are almost entirely active through our imagination, meaning that we create and recall imagery as a way of giving meaning to our dream and nightmare experiences. The phrase, "a picture is worth a thousand words" absolutely applies here. Imagery is a powerful language here on earth.

The cat may not have actually been a cat. It is most likely to me that she was an energetic astral being but that's difficult to understand in the waking world, so my mind-body-energy system worked with her to create the imagery of a cat in order to help me comprehend what I had encountered in the dreamspace.

We are the creators of our realities and the same goes for the dreamspace as well.

I believe these experiences in childhood with the ghouls and the astral cat to be "real" in that they were things my energy encountered on another layer of existence and that I remembered as a nightmare.

Application

I don't remember what I thought about this nightmare at the time, but I do know that it was an incredibly powerful experience because I viscerally remember it all these years later. If a child told me this dream today, I'd suggest to their parents to guide the child in identifying what they fear, what might be causing that fear, and find a way to resolve it or provide the child with clarity.

Chased by Witches

This is the earliest recurring nightmare that I can recall. I think I remember telling my mom about it a few times but there was no real understanding that came from it, just a sense that everyone had nightmares and I needed to learn how to either suppress them or shake them off. Today, I've gone back with an interpretation that resonates for me and it may resonate with many people because, in my work as a dream and nightmare interpreter, I've come across many individuals who have encountered witches in their dream space.

Elements

1. Forest: A natural space, a collection of trees. The natural spaces within myself. Trees can sometimes represent the totality of our spirit structure or the Axis Mundi (the concept of the World Tree that is described in many cultures). The roots of the Axis Mundi represent our ancestry, the underworld and where we come from. The trunk represents the strong linear timeline of our current human experience and everyday activities. And the branches represent our universal, spiritual, or religious beliefs and what lies beyond our physical experience. Trees may also be related to the social concept of a "family tree," (this last one resonates most for me in this dream).

2. Witches: Beings we're taught to fear (taught to me from

the Catholic church). Powerful women.

3. Running or Being Chased: Represents either, "What am I running from" or "What am I afraid will catch up to me?" Both apply to me in this dream.

4. Smoke: An alarming smell associated with something burning. A trigger. Haziness.

5. Fire: An all-consuming power only doused by water. Alchemization.

Emotions

Fear, panic, avoidance

Interpretation

I see this dream as both an exploration of my natural inner spaces and of my family tree or ancestry. The forest is dark and foggy just like the sense of confusion I had as a kid combined with the familial narrative of avoidance. The witches represent something that I was told I should fear and I *do* fear it because I'm a child and I believe what I'm told. I was taught that witches were evil and in the dream I was afraid of the dark, evil thing catching up to me. I was running away from my fear. The witches in this dream (which was recurrent) could have been a very early, more human version of the leviathan.

I would add another layer onto this. Witches were persecuted and, during the witch hunts of the Middle Ages, many people became fearful of their neighbors. The Church made it a priority to control information and sow distrust to solidify their sense of control for men's profit. The vast majority of people accused of witchcraft were innocent. At the time, anyone who practiced medicinal healing or shared words of self-empowerment was identified as a threat to the Church who wanted to monopolize not only the religious space, but everything to do with survival of the human species. Any individual not affiliated with the Church who had the power to perform "miracles," (acts of healing such as concocting healing herbal teas, prescribing poultices, and sharing basic sanitation knowledge) was persecuted.

In my dream, I now see the witches as a representation of all the powerful women who have come before me. They're chasing me down not to harm me, but to help me. Fire can be seen as a cleansing force and in this dream the witches wanted to help me burn down the family system (represented by the trees in the forest) so we could all finally acknowledge our shit and process our individual traumas. Fire is a destructive element, yes, but it's also an alchemizing one. Like prairie burns, sometimes we need to wipe the slate clean so that we can start over again. But I was taught to fear change as a child instead of how to embrace it, so the dream remained a nightmare.

Application

If you're a parent of children with nightmares, discussing the nightmares with your child can be a great way to help them integrate difficult concepts and topics they might be stuck on.

Sleep Paralysis

Scientific knowledge and studies on dreams are in their relative infancy when compared to the physical sciences and sleep paralysis has been studied even less. What follows is my own personal research, personal beliefs, and personal experiences. I encourage you to do your own research.

In very simplistic terms, the leading theory for physical paralysis during sleep begins with a neurotransmitter called gamma-aminobutyric acid (GABA) and an amino acid called glycine.[1] During sleep, these two compounds work together to turn the body into a limp noodle which prevents us from acting out our dreams and potentially causing ourselves bodily harm. From a physical perspective only, paralysis during sleep can be seen as an evolutionary mechanism designed to minimize physical injury.

Most people have little or no recollection of this nightly experience. However, some individuals begin to "wake up" or step into conscious awareness before the physical effects of the paralysis have worn off. This can be a jarring experience for unsuspecting dreamers and can initiate a fear response throughout our mind-body-energy system. I believe that fear-based sleep paralysis occurs when the subconscious mind intentionally initiates conscious aware-

---

1. Brooks, P. L., & Peever, J. H. (2012, July 18). *Identification of the Transmitter and Receptor Mechanisms Responsible for REM Sleep Paralysis*. Journal of Neuroscience. https://doi.org/10.1523/JNEUROSCI.0482-12.2012

ness while in the paralyzed liminal space between dreaming and wakefulness. It does this because when we are in that space, we encounter our completely unfiltered selves and if there's anything we've been fearing or suppressing we are confronted with it there. Our subconscious mind knows that we cannot ignore our fears forever, we must take action to move through them but we cannot take action on that which we do not see nor acknowledge.

Sleep paralysis demons are just our fears personified. They're the parts of ourselves that we have been feeding with fear until they grow into something so profound that they take on a nightmarish form. They're the parts of you that need to be seen and held and acknowledged. They represent something repressed, something difficult, something that has grown steadily over time so much that it has taken on the figure of something alive. They represent the fears we have given life to.

Sleep paralysis demons can take on different forms the more we acknowledge and work with them. I have three main forms of note:

1. The spider-like, venom-dripping demon on the ceiling. To me, spiders are not only something creepy and unpleasant but represent the weavers of stories and memories (visualized through the creation of their webs). This sleep paralysis demon represents the fear I had of stepping outside of my family system and into a world where I could begin weaving my own story. I was very fearful of what would happen if I let go of what I had been told and discovered things for myself. It also represents the observation of what had woven my story thus far. This demon showed me (on a very subconscious level that I have broken down after the fact) that I needed to become

the weaver of my own story.

2. The minions of dread from Afghanistan. My fears exploded at the time because I found myself once again submerged in a traumatic environment full of life and death scenarios. The minions represent my numerous fears at this point.

3. The veiled woman. The spider-like creature morphs. At first it dons a cloak, becoming more human and more recognizable—a reflection of my growing acknowledgments and familiarity with my own fears. It turns its "face" towards me, and I see that it's just a yawning hole. The hole is a void representing the unknown. I am now face-to-face with what has remained "unknown" within me—the truth that I have hidden from myself of who originally caused me harm. The intricate lacework and thin veil represent the thinning layer separating those memories from my full acknowledgment. She's a mourning widow because she represents the loss of my childhood innocence.

Note: Over the last couple of years, I have encountered other forms of sleep paralysis without fear. These new (to me) forms of sleep paralysis are encounters with my soul—what's left after clearing out the fear. They have led to full out-of-body experiences which have been incredibly beautiful and have had a profoundly positive impact on my life. For more on these other forms of sleep paralysis and OBE adventures, check out my podcast *The Axis Channel*.

Recurring Themes in Minnesota

Being Chased

A chasing nightmare usually indicates the feeling of wanting to run away from something that we fear or the feeling that something is catching up to us. In either case, the nightmare is trying to help us identify the fear. This is where the details can be helpful.

Some of my chasing dreams include:

- Being chased by a mob of bloodthirsty people. A mob is a group of aligned people who are typically acting out their fear, anger, or frustration in a disruptive way. In the context of my nightmares, they represent the concept of social norms and cultural narratives. At the time that I was experiencing these nightmares I had a deep-seated fear that breaking out of the family system was going to incite my family to come after me in a very negative way. The nightmare was asking me to acknowledge and let go of my fear of unconforming.

- Being chased by crocodiles. These ancient, cold-blooded creatures hide and hunt underwater. The crocodiles were reminiscent of my leviathan and the old truths that lay in wait under the surface of my emotions (water) and memories but represented lesser fears.

- Being chased by witches. I had a few of these nightmares

here and there again as an adult which reminded me of the ones I'd had as a child.

Feelings of Shame and Self-Loathing

Emotions are the key element of dream and nightmare interpretation. In these nightmares I was showing myself exactly what I felt about myself and the innate beliefs that were keeping me "stuck." I was showing myself the inner narratives I needed to unpack and redefine. My therapist then helped me dig into the source of those emotions.

Enacting Violence

Violence in the dreamspace, whether you're hurting and/or causing suffering for others or you, yourself, are being hurt, are a visualized expression of anger and pain. They can help us identify where we feel hurt, who we feel hurt by, and where our anger towards others is directed.

For example, if someone stabs you in the back in a nightmare you might ask yourself where in waking life you feel like you've been "stabbed in the back," which is a phrase we use for being betrayed and the pain of losing trust in someone. Another example is being shot in a nightmare which usually represents a quick but powerful wound. If we are the one enacting violence it's almost always a call to reflect on who we feel like we are hurting in our waking lives (usually with words or actions).

People in Dreams

People in our dreamspace are usually just parts of ourselves that we're interacting with. Yes, they can look like someone we know in waking life, but usually a part of ourselves dons the mask of another person so that we may interact with a concept that they represent. Another person's imagery in a dream could represent the relationship and connection to them or, more often, what we associate them with.

For example, if I dream about a spiritual friend, I might be dreaming about the part of me that relates to spirituality—not the friend themself. If I dream about my father-in-law, I'm most likely interacting with the idea of being goofy, loving, and good with kids. If I dream about my husband, I'm probably dreaming about the part of me that shows up in romantic partnership.

The Basement Shower

If you've read to the end of this book, then you already know the context of this but let's break down some of the imagery further.

Elements

1. Basement: Found in houses in the dream space which usually represent the foundational structure of our minds. Each room in a physical house serves a different purpose, therefore, each room in a psychological house in the dreamspace holds a different conceptual area of life. For example, each level of a house can indicate different overarching themes: the main floor of a home is usually where our day-to-day activities take place and is most often associated with everyday life, the upper floors or attic of a home can represent our "higher" beliefs, spirituality, or what we think is "above" or beyond the human experience, and the basement of a home can be related to ancestry or our "underworld" and sometimes the things we pack away into basement storage or the proverbial "skeletons in the closet."

2. Shower: A facility for cleaning oneself.

3. No Walls or the Lack of Walls: Lack of structure and the feeling of vulnerability. Openness.

4. Clothing: Represents how we express ourselves, what we

take onto ourselves, or how other people see us but in the context of this nightmare it felt like more of a safety feature or something that was covering my vulnerability.

5. Hateful Presence Watching at the Top of the Stairs: The part of me that didn't want me to explore this. The part of me that held all of the self-hatred and loathing but could do nothing but watch me unpack it all.

Emotions

Vulnerable, watched, judged, terrified, dirty

Interpretation

Again, this is more indicative of a memory than anything, but the scene does help me see that I was looking into my own proverbial basement and readying myself to unbox some of the skeletons I'd packed away long ago. I was getting ready to "clean" myself of them, but this space still felt dirty as evidenced by the dirt swirling in the water on the floor—there was more work to do before I would be ready to clear out and wash away those memories. I needed to release any self-disgust I was holding onto.

It was an incredibly vulnerable space for me to be within myself and I was still afraid to be vulnerable. The part of me that feared what I was doing (digging up the old memories) stood at the top of the stairs trying to intimidate me into forgetting about it.

A Brief Compendium of Common Nightmares

B efore diving into the nightmare definitions below, please ensure that you have read "A Brief Note on Interpretation" at the beginning of the *Exploration and Interpretation* section.

Dreams and nightmares are an expression of our internal conversation. They show us exactly what's going on under the surface of our everyday thoughts and feelings. This makes the observation and interpretation of dreams and nightmares a great way to connect with the full authenticity of ourselves.

This Compendium contains brief descriptions of common nightmares and their meanings as I've discovered through my work as a dream and nightmare interpreter. Each of the definitions has been paired with a series of questions for deep, personal exploration which I encourage you to use as an agent of change in your waking life. Like a dream dictionary, this Compendium should only be used as a starting point as you discover your own meanings and interpretations.

Apocalyptic and Post-Apocalyptic

These nightmares can range anywhere from nuclear fallout-type apocalypses to the simple sense of knowing that something fundamental has changed in your nightmare's surroundings. They often indicate that a part of our lives is either currently experiencing destruction or that we are already living in the aftermath of that destruction.

Apocalyptic nightmares ask us to acknowledge the full scope of what is currently being destroyed in our lives or what has recently been destroyed. Destruction is a natural part of life—a part of the cycle of creation—and always leads to the growth of something new. Once something in our lives has been destroyed, our capacity for something new expands and encourages us to rebuild a new foundation with the knowledge of our previous experiences. These nightmares ask us to let go of what no longer serves us and move forward in a new way.

Apocalyptic nightmares can also be a way of expressing grief and loss for what was destroyed while in the safety of the dreamspace, especially if we don't feel like we have the ability to openly express those emotions in waking life.

Questions for Exploration

- What in my life feels completely upended right now or what I am afraid will feel upending?

- In what area of my life am I experiencing survival mode?

- If an "apocalypse" or upending scenario is imminent (like losing a job, an unexpected pregnancy, experiencing familial fall-out, etc.), how can you best set yourself up for success?

Anxiety

Nightmares in which you feel anxiety or panic can help you identify where in your life you are either currently feeling anxiety or where you have experienced anxiety in the past.

Anxiety nightmares ask us to identify and acknowledge where we are feeling anxiety in our waking lives, no matter how small or insignificant it may seem. When we acknowledge the cause(s) of our anxiety we can disrupt the old narrative of fear and release the need to worry. The more we disrupt the old narrative, the more we can shape a new one and encourage the anxiety to dissolve over time.

Sometimes, our anxiety nightmares may not be indicating the current feeling of anxiety but we can still experience them because something that used to trigger feelings of anxiety may have occurred in our waking lives and these nightmares are simply still in the healing process of those old narratives.

Questions for Exploration

- Where in my life am I feeling anxiety or have I recently experienced an old trigger for anxiety?

- How can I acknowledge those feelings of anxiety and disrupt the old narrative?

- What tools in my psychological/healing toolbox can help me process this anxiety?

Bathrooms and Using the Toilet

Bathroom dreams and nightmares represent the process of releasing what no longer serves us. Using the toilet is an everyday, extremely important function for our physical bodies and the conceptual action behind it is often used to convey how we release old thoughts, limiting narratives or outdated information in the dreamspace.

When we have nightmares or negative dreams about not being able to find a toilet, running out of toilet paper, or being watched by a crowd of people while on the toilet, we encounter the specific fears we have around the concept of releasing something (i.e. not finding the right space or time to release it, fear of not being able to feel clean after releasing it, and the fear of being judged by others in how we are releasing it). Each of these nightmares is asking us to acknowledge and work through our fears of letting go and moving on.

Questions for Exploration

- What have I been holding onto past its expiration?

- Why have I been holding onto this?

- What am I afraid will happen if I release it?

- How can I help myself begin to let go?

Car Trouble

Car trouble nightmares may explore issues with starting the vehicle, getting into a crash, someone stealing the vehicle or even careening around in the backseat with a crazy driver behind the wheel. They represent how we feel like we're moving through life and the current state of our life journey.

Cars are vehicles that help us move from point A to point B and most often represent the concept of movement in the dreamspace. Movement and growth (physically, psychologically, emotionally and spiritually) are necessary facets of the human experience. These nightmares show us the fears that stand in the way of our growth and movement.

Questions for Exploration
- If you're unable to start the car in the nightmare, do you feel like you're stuck or unable to get started on a project or other area of waking life? Are you afraid of getting started?

- If you crashed the car in the nightmare or almost crashed, do you feel like you're going to "crash and burn" somewhere in waking life or have you been brought to a stop by something?

- If your car was stolen in the nightmare, do you feel like something has been taken from you or that something you wanted was never offered to you?

- If someone else is driving the car in a nightmare, do you feel like someone else is "driving" you through life? Do you trust that person? Are you ready to get in the front seat and drive yourself?

Chasing or Being Chased

These nightmares are often in the latter context where we're either being chased by something or someone or we're running away from something we don't want to acknowledge, but they can also be experienced as nightmares when we're chasing after something we desperately want that we seemingly can never reach.

When we're being chased in a nightmare we're asking ourselves to acknowledge what we're afraid will catch up to us or why we're running away from something. These nightmares are asking us to stop running, embrace our inner bravery and courage, and turn to meet the thing that we've been avoiding.

When we're chasing after something we seem to never reach it's time to get clear about why we're chasing it. These nightmares also provide us with an opportunity to ask ourselves why we're unhappy with what we have in the present moment.

Questions for Exploration

- What have I been running from or what have I been avoiding?

- How can I embrace bravery and courage to turn and meet it?

- Why do I chase after something I can seemingly never attain? Do I need to continue chasing it?

Cheating

Cheating nightmares are very common though they rarely indicate that your partner is actually cheating on you. Most often, these nightmares explore a waking-life scenario where you feel like you have been cheated or betrayed.

The people in our dreamspaces usually represent the concepts we associate with them, not necessarily our relationships with them in waking life. Cheating nightmares often use the imagery of a partner or significant other to convey how deeply the feeling of being cheated or betrayed is rooted. These nightmares ask us to identify where we feel like we have been wronged so that we can communicate that feeling and find resolution.

As an example, let's say a man dreamt of his wife cheating on him with his boss. He knows that his wife isn't cheating in waking life and asks himself where in waking life he feels like he is being cheated on. Immediately, the imagery of his boss catches his attention, and he realizes that the promotion his good friend and coworker recently received is bothering him more than he's been allowing himself to realize. He believes he should have received the promotion instead. The nightmare is using his wife's imagery to convey how deeply betrayed he feels by his boss. After acknowledging this and fully feeling through the betrayal, the man calmly acknowledges his options such as requesting a raise, discussing why he was not promoted with his boss, or even spiffing up his resume and moving on.

Questions for Exploration

- Where in my life do I feel like I'm being cheated?

- Have I not received something I feel like I truly deserved?

Death and Dying

These nightmares show us what we fear to lose or what we feel like we have already lost. They can also show us our own fears of death and the dying process.

Nightmares that depict death (our own or someone else's) are asking us to come to terms with the concept of loss. Endings are a part of life and learning how to accept loss with grace is a skill many of us will work at our whole lives. These nightmares can show us exactly what or who we are afraid of losing, even if it is a part of ourselves. When we acknowledge our fear we can begin to work on accepting impermanence.

Questions for Exploration

- What or who am I afraid of losing and why am I afraid of losing it/them?

- Where in my life am I afraid of loss? Why?

- What do I believe happens when I lose someone or lose something? Is this true or is it only a fear?

Drowning

These nightmares often indicate the feeling of being completely overwhelmed.

The element of water is almost always associated with emotion in the dreamspace. Drowning nightmares ask us to acknowledge where we feel overwhelmed in our waking lives. Once we acknowledge the area that feels overwhelming we can take action to alleviate some of the stress, ask for help in coming to the surface, or find another avenue to move through the situation.

Questions for Exploration
- Where do I feel like I'm "drowning" in waking life?

- Where in my life do I feel overwhelmed?

- How can I seek help and support through this?

Earthquake

Earthquakes come from within the Earth's crust which is the foundational structure we live on here at the surface of our planet. These nightmares indicate that a foundational part of our lives is either currently shaking up or that a foundational shake up occurred in the past (and is currently affecting us).

The concept of foundations can relate to our family structure, core belief system, home life, source of income, etc. Earthquake nightmares ask us to acknowledge which part of our psychological foundation is experiencing a shake up so that we may show up for ourselves and find a way through it. Alternatively, if a part of your foundation was shaken in the past, these nightmares could indicate that something is currently triggering the fear of another foundational "earthquake" which can be a great opportunity to work with the old wound and continue to heal the narrative.

Questions for Exploration

- Where in my life do I feel like my foundation is crumbling?

- What grounding force that I've been relying on is slipping away?

- How can I help myself land as softly as possible?

- What trigger in life has recently reminded me of an old foundational "earthquake?"

Failing (Something or Someone)

Nightmares in which we fail to pass a test, fail one of our loved ones, or experience failure in another way explore not only what we have taken responsibility for but what we have become emotionally attached to.

Failing means that there was a task we took responsibility for or something that we cared about. It's ok to fail most things in life and every failure is a learning opportunity. These nightmares show us where we need to give ourselves more grace and forgiveness. They can also show us where we are attached to something or to a particular outcome.

Questions for Exploration

- Where do I feel like a failure or what do I feel like I have failed?

- What can I learn from my failure?

- Where can I find room for grace and self-forgiveness?

- What outcome or thing am I attached to? Why am I attached to it?

Falling

Falling nightmares explore the feeling of uncertainty, where we feel like our lives are "falling" out of control, or where we're coming face to face with a reality we've been avoiding.

These nightmares are an opportunity to stop clinging to control and to embrace the unknown. If we've been avoiding something in our waking lives, it's time to acknowledge it and allow ourselves to step through it so that we may emerge once more on the other side.

Questions for Exploration

- What am I clinging to that's slipping away?

- Do I feel like I'm out of control somewhere in my life?

- Am I afraid of the uncertainty of something?

- How can I help myself to see that this is momentary and there's always a way to climb back up?

Illness

Having an illness in a nightmare indicates that we've been emotionally holding onto something that is starting to fester within our mind-body-energy system.

The body holds onto our traumas and can help us point out where we're storing old memories and difficulties through illness nightmares. These nightmares help us to see that there's something unresolved. They're a call to acknowledge, rest, recuperate, and heal. If you've been holding a grudge, still feeling angry about something in the past, or haven't' healed a memory that is still consuming you these nightmares are an indication to start walking your healing pathway.

Sometimes, the part of the body that is ill in the nightmare can help us identify the memory or area of our life that is being pointed out. If we have a throat illness in the nightmare it may be related to speaking our truth or feeling free to say what we need to say. If we have an illness in our legs that prevents us from walking in the nightmare it may be something that's getting in the way of how we move through life. If we have a lung illness or trouble breathing in the nightmare it might be related to "breathing room" or an inability to "catch our breath" in life.

Questions for Exploration

- What part of the body is ill in the nightmare? Think about that part's function. Does it translate to a difficult feeling or memory in your life?

- What have you been holding onto?

- What experience or memory does not feel fully healed?

Lateness or Running Late

Nightmares in which we are late for something usually indicate that we feel left behind or that we missed out on something. They explore feelings of regret.

These nightmares ask us to acknowledge where regret exists within us so that we can begin the healing process of letting go. Regret is an opportunity to consciously find thankfulness in our present moment. There will always be more opportunities in the future. In this human existence we can't have it all—literally, we do not have the time to experience every opportunity in a single lifetime—so let go of the past and meet yourself where you're at.

Questions for Exploration

- What do I regret? Why am I still attached to it?

- Do I feel like I've been left behind? How can I strike out on my own path?

- How can I let go of the limiting narratives that place unwanted expectations upon me?

Losing (Something/an Object)

These nightmares of losing something differ from death and dying nightmares in that they usually relate to objects. Losing something in a nightmare usually indicates that we feel uncertain about a part of ourselves or that a part of ourselves is struggling to come forward.

The purpose or function of the object in question can provide you with more clarity on what you feel like you're losing or what you cannot find. Some of the most common losing nightmares I've encountered include lost cell phones (struggling to effectively communicate or interact with the wider world), purses or bags (experiencing a loss of personal identity or something important/functional in their life), and cars (feeling stuck or unable to move forward). Once we acknowledge the area in which we are struggling or what feels uncertain, we can take action to consciously seek out what we have "lost."

Questions for Exploration

- What part of myself or my life feels like it's struggling right now?

- What do I feel like I cannot find in life?

- Do I feel confusion about myself or who I am? How can I rediscover myself?

(Being) Lost

When we are the ones who are lost in a nightmare, we are often exploring feelings of confusion and uncertainty.

Being lost in a nightmare indicates a state of "analysis paralysis" or the fear of making decisions and striking out on our own path. They're accompanied by the internal statement, "I don't know what to do," and the desire for someone to tell us what to do. These nightmares are an opportunity to get in the driver's seat and start enacting our free will. There is nothing you "should" be doing; there is only what you choose to do. The details and function of the surroundings in the nightmare can provide more detail.

Questions for Exploration

- Where am I struggling to make a decision?

- Why am I afraid of making a decision?

- Where do I feel confused or "lost" in life?

- Do I feel like I "should" be doing something? Why do I think that?

- How can I branch out and make my own choice?

Nakedness

Nightmares in which we're naked explore the concept of vulnerability.

These nightmares are incredibly beneficial! It takes a lot of inner strength and bravery to openly show or display our vulnerabilities. These nightmares are an opportunity to acknowledge our humanity, show our authenticity, and build trust amongst others and within ourselves. Wherever there is vulnerability there is often either an old wound or a memory of watching another be wounded in relation to that vulnerability. It's time to heal that wound or belief we formed around the vulnerability.

Questions for Exploration

- Where in my life do I feel most vulnerable?

- Why do I feel vulnerable? Was I hurt in this part of my life, or did I witness another being hurt?

- How can I hold this vulnerability and begin to acknowledge it as a strength?

Teeth Falling Out

Teeth nightmares can vary quite a bit but when teeth fall out in a nightmare it signals loss or feeling like we're losing something.

Teeth are not only used to bite and chew our food but are used as a defense mechanism in wild animals. When we think of large, carnivorous predators we think about their teeth. Losing teeth in a nightmare may be related to feeling unable to process what's happening in our lives right now (associated with the action of chewing our food/chewing things over) or feeling unable to defend ourselves.

Questions for Exploration

- Where do I feel like I'm losing the ability to defend myself?

- Where do I feel like I'm losing the ability to process or "chew things over?"

- Where do I feel like I'm incapable of standing up for myself?

- Where do I feel loss, in general?

Tornados

These nightmares, like apocalyptic nightmares, depict the ever-present concept of death and rebirth or endings and new beginnings. Tornado nightmares can show us where we feel like a part of our lives is being destroyed.

However, tornados travel along a linear path and may not represent something as all-encompassing as an apocalypse. For example, let's say a company is laying off many employees. Some of the employees might have apocalypse dreams following the lay-off because of the wide-reaching impact. On the other hand, if a single employee was laid off, that employee would be more likely to experience a tornado nightmare than a full-on apocalyptic scenario. In either case, nightmares of total destruction signal an ending which leads to a clean slate for a new beginning.

Questions for Exploration

- What experience or area of life feels like its being destroyed right now?

- Where do I feel like my life has been turned upside down?

- If you saw a tornado in the distance in your nightmare, do you see a potential "disaster" coming towards you in waking life?

- How can you begin to rebuild this foundational part of your life anew?

(Being) Trapped

Being trapped in a nightmare often signals a belief that we're locked into something we didn't want in the first place or something we no longer want.

These nightmares encourage us to acknowledge what we truly want, and that change is needed. It's time to let go and move on. We are never truly locked into anything; there is always a choice.

Questions for Exploration

- Where do I feel like I'm trapped?

- What might I not actually want?

- How can I be honest with myself and find a way out of this situation?

Tsunami

Water, again, almost always symbolizes emotion. Tsunami nightmares explore the fear we have of being totally consumed by overwhelming emotion.

These nightmares are great warning signals that can help us prepare for emotionally difficult times. Instead of shutting down, they present us with an opportunity to connect with our support system and get our processing methods in place before the tsunami "hits."

Questions for Exploration

- What in my life feels like it's going to be emotionally overloading and is coming in fast?

- What can I do to prepare for the emotional overload in a healthy way?

- Who can I ask for help?

Violence

Nightmares with physical violence show us where we feel hurt, how we may be hurting ourselves, or if we feel like we're causing others pain.

These nightmares are common, and most people will have at least one at some point in their lives. Most often, they show us how we feel about pain or where we feel hurt. The specifics of the violence can further help us identify where we're feeling that pain. Once we acknowledge where pain exists, we can being to heal it.

Questions for Exploration
- Where in my life do I feel like I am being hurt?

- Where in my life do I feel like I am hurting others?

- Am I causing my own pain?

- What can I do to stop hurting myself or others, or step away from people who are hurting me?

- How can I begin to heal?

Visitations from the Deceased
(in a negative sense)

Visitations are dreams or nightmares where we are visited by passed loved ones. These dreams and nightmares typically have a profound sense of gravity to them where we wake up and think, "WHOA! That was a powerful dream." Most often, they're wonderful experiences where the spirits of the departed stop by to cheer us on, say hello, or just show us that they're still with us. But sometimes visitations can feel like nightmares and when they do it usually means there's something we have left unresolved with the deceased.

For clarity, when the true spirits of our loved ones visit us, it is *always* a positive, uplifting, or neutral experience and is classified as a dream. When we experience a negative visitation, a nightmare, the deceased is a figment of our imagination or dreamspace, not the spirit of the departed, and it is always a psychological experience designed to help us process any guilt or unresolved emotions that have lingered after their parting. Visitation nightmares are an opportunity to begin the acknowledgment and self-forgiveness process.

Questions for Exploration
- What do I feel is unresolved with this deceased individual?

- How can I hold space for myself to find internal resolution?

Acknowledgments

There are many people who have contributed to my healing experience and this book would not exist without them.

Brandon, thank you so much for believing in me, for loving me, and for showing me how good life can truly be. Thank you for reading and rereading and re-rereading this book through all of its iterations. You are my biggest supporter and the brightest star in the great expanse of my dreamspace. I love you to the unending end and back and I'm beyond excited to explore the rest of this magickal existence with you.

To my editor and dear friend, James, thank you so much for holding this book with me. Your words of encouragement, hilarious anecdotes, incredibly honest and supportive feedback and deep work that took this book to the next level have my heart bursting with gratitude. Thank you for contributing to this incredibly meaningful project.

To my siblings, thank you for being a part of my life. I hope that you continue to grow and heal and love in your own ways.

Julia, Jason, Aaron, Caitlin, Aurora, Alex, and Jess, I love each of you so very much. Thank you all for showing me endless versions of love and support but, most of all, thank you for showing me how beautiful a family experience can truly be.

Rachel, you truly are a bright light in the story of my life. Thank you for helping me when I didn't know what else to do, for trusting me when I was still learning how to trust myself, and for guiding me through some of the darkest moments in my existence. You are an amazing soul and one of the greatest healers I have ever known.

To Lauren, Hansie, Ingrid, Adam, Amanda, and James, your laughter, friendship, and support is truly wonderful.

Alea, thank you for witnessing me, encouraging me, and for being the friend I can say the craziest, weirdest shit to. We definitely know each other outside of this human experience.

Aly, our weekly chats have kept me sane. Thank you for your supportive encouragement, honesty, and understanding along the way. It helps to have a friend who knows.

And finally, to all the amazing pets in my life: Daruk, Bear, Lilly, Rowdy (yes, even Rowdy), Olive, Ty, Ada, Bernie, Roody-Roo, Zennie Girl, and Mara, thank you for sharing such pure forms of love with me. I will always scratch your tummies when asked, snuggle you close when your breath isn't too stinky, and happily pick up your literal shit because this love is endless.

Books that Changed my Life

Andrews, Ted: *Animal Speak*

Bryson, Bill: *A Walk in the Woods*

Coelho, Paulo: *The Alchemist*

Crisp, Tony: *Dream Dictionary*

Earley, Jay, PhD: *Self-Therapy: A Step-by-Step Guide to Creating Wholeness Using IFS, A Cutting-Edge Psychotherapy*

Gray, Kyle: *Divine Masters, Ancient Wisdom*

Hadfield, Col. Chris: *An Astronaut's Guide to Life on Earth*

Hof, Wim, and Elissa Epel, PhD: *The Wim Hof Method: Activate Your Full Human Potential*

Honda, Ken: *Happy Money*

Jemisin, N.K.: *The Fifth Season*

Jemisin, N.K.: *The Obelisk Gate*

Jemisin, N.K.: *The Stone Sky*

King, Stephen: *On Writing: A Memoir of the Craft*

Miller, David: *AWOL on the Appalachian Trail*

Rowling, J.K.: *Harry Potter and the Chamber of Secrets*

Rowling, J.K.: *Harry Potter and the Deathly Hallows*

Rowling, J.K.: *Harry Potter and the Goblet of Fire*

Rowling, J.K.: *Harry Potter and the Half-Blood Prince*

Rowling, J.K.: *Harry Potter and the Order of the Phoenix*

Rowling, J.K.: *Harry Potter and the Prisoner of Azkaban*

Rowling, J.K.: *Harry Potter and the Sorcerer's Stone*

Salvatore, R.A.: *Exile: The Legend of Drizzt*

Salvatore, R.A.: *Homeland: The Legend of Drizzt*

Salvatore, R.A.: *Sojourn: The Legend of Drizzt*

Scovel Shinn, Florence: *The Complete Works of Florence Scovel Shinn*

Scully, Nicki: *Sekhmet: Transformation in the Belly of the Goddess*

Tolkien, J.R.R.: *The Fellowship of the Ring*

Tolkien, J.R.R.: *The Hobbit*

Tolkien, J.R.R.: *The Return of the King*

Tolkien, J.R.R.: *The Two Towers*

Tolle, Eckhart: *A New Earth: Awakening to Your Life's Purpose*

Wangyal, Tenzin (Rinpoche): *The Tibetan Yogas of Dream and Sleep*

Standalone Titles:

The Bhagavad Gita (Attributed to Vyasa)

The Hermetica (Attributed to Hermes Trismegistus)

www.ingramcontent.com/pod-product-compliance
Lightning Source LLC
Chambersburg PA
CBHW010938120626
46554CB00008B/2514